GREATER HARTFORD
MEMORIES

A PHOTOGRAPHIC HISTORY OF THE 1800s THROUGH THE 1930s

Hartford Courant

The following organizations have contributed greatly to this project:

Historical Society of East Hartford

Jewish Historical Society of Greater Hartford • The Mark Twain House & Museum

Special Thanks

Section Introductions — Jesse Leavenworth
Editing — Tim Castillo, Mikala Kane, Marc O'Connell, Scott Powers
Andrew S. Julien, Publisher & Editor-in-Chief

On the Cover

A view of crowds on the State Capitol grounds, Hartford, circa late 1800s. COURTESY B. R. BECKWITH COLLECTION

Published by Pediment Publishing,
a division of The Pediment Group, Inc.

www.pediment.com

Printed in Canada

Foreword

The story of Connecticut is the story of our nation. It's a story about dreamers and doers, of triumph and tragedy. It's a story about people united by the notion that hope and imagination can carry almost any day.

In the pages of this book, you will see people you've heard of and others you haven't. You'll see scenes and buildings that are still familiar today while others have faded from memory. Taken as a whole, they tell a story of a place and a people. Linger for a moment on the fierce look in the eyes of Harriet Beecher Stowe or the glint in the smiles of dairy workers at A. C. Petersen Farms.

We open with a chapter on street scenes, highlighting the architecture of a city heralded for its beauty by Mark Twain. Then we're taken back to an era when getting from one place to another was no less important than it is today, but the means were very different, an era of railways and steamboats, trams and trolley cars. In Chapter Three, we meet the business owners and shopkeepers that lined the city's streets.

Then we get to the heart of the Yankee spirit—innovation and invention. Hartford has long been a cradle of discovery and progress, home to makers of firearms, bicycles, airplane engines, and more. Protecting the growing wealth of the nation through the insurance industry became another pillar of Hartford commerce. In Chapter Five we move on to schools and education.

Next up are the police officers and firefighters who have long worked to keep our homes and streets safe. Chapter Seven charts the dramatic shifts in Connecticut's communities, from a state that revolved largely around its Congregational churches to a rich tapestry of cultures and faiths. Finally, this volume concludes with the games, fairs, picnics, and festivals that brought people together to compete and laugh, to share a special moment with family or friends.

The *Hartford Courant* has long had the privilege of telling Connecticut's stories (since 1764, in fact!), and we are proud to bring you this visual history as well.

Table of Contents

CHAPTER ONE

Views and Street Scenes

A time-traveling Connecticut Yankee from the late 1800s would not be lost in modern Hartford. The Soldiers and Sailors Memorial Arch, dedicated in 1886, would be familiar, along with the golden dome of the nearby state Capitol, completed in 1879. Our traveler might wonder, however, where the Park River went. Certainly, the city's vertical profile and ribbons of converging highways would amaze.

The photographs here cover a time of extraordinary growth and change in Connecticut's capital city and the region. From 1870 to 1950, the population of Hartford and its suburbs rose from about 60,000 to more than 300,000, fueled by a flourishing insurance market and manufacturers such as Colt Industries that sold products worldwide.

Business profits made Hartford a Gilded Age hub and produced commercial and civic buildings and homes of elegant style and grand scale. Consider the old Post Office and Custom House on City Hall Square, the Second Empire-style Connecticut Mutual Life Insurance Company building at Main and Pearl streets, and of course, the state Capitol building, among the nation's most intricate and distinct.

For many years, Connecticut had two capital cities, New Haven and Hartford. In 1873, residents chose Hartford as the seat of state government. Seeking a spot for the Capitol building, the legislature settled on land that had been the original home of Trinity College.

The Capitol's architecture is high-Victorian Gothic with Italianate and classical elements. Initially projected at $900,000, the cost wound up at about $2.5 million.

The city that longtime resident Mark Twain once called the nation's most beautiful also features homes built with a focus on quality materials and supreme craftsmanship, including the cluster of houses at Farmington Avenue and Forest Street called Nook Farm.

Nook Farm neighbors and friends were a groundbreaking group who often held all-night, heated discussions about the issues of the day. Isabella Beecher Hooker, sister of author Harriet Beecher Stowe, lived with husband John on Forest Street. Isabella was an early feminist, abolitionist, and suffragette. She also was devoted to "spirit conversations" with the dead, sometimes hosting multiple mediums at her home.

People with far less money and time for such pursuits lived in neighborhoods such as Front Street near the Connecticut River. In apartment buildings with clotheslines strung from back landings, the region's demographics quickly turned from mostly white and protestant to the wide diversity that characterizes the region today.

Front Street and other neighborhoods where immigrants formed ethnic enclaves have declined and risen again, and urban renewal and natural disasters such as the flood of 1936 have erased parts of Hartford and its suburbs. The flood displaced about 10,000 people and also prompted the diversion and covering of the Park River from Bushnell Park to the Connecticut River.

But throughout the region, streetscapes from the turn of the last century survive. Stand today at Main and West Main streets in New Britain and compare the view to the photo here of the Gates Building and City Hall.

The landscape of central Connecticut has changed much over the past 150 years, but much more than remnants of the past remain.

OPPOSITE: Bushnell Park, downtown Hartford. 1910s. COURTESY HARRIET BEECHER STOWE CENTER / #NO. 1

ABOVE: A postcard of Main and Asylum Streets looking north, Hartford, 1862.
COURTESY CONNECTICUT STATE LIBRARY / #PICTURE GROUP 800 POSTCARDS, CONNECTICUT HARTFORD-KILLINGWORTH BOX 6

ABOVE RIGHT: State and Commerce Streets lined with horse-drawn wagons, Hartford, about 1869.
COURTESY CONNECTICUT STATE LIBRARY / #PICTURE GROUP 400 HARTFORD COLLECTION 1885-1936, RESTAURANTS-TROLLEYS, BOX 5 OF 5

RIGHT: Streets decorated in celebration of Battle Flag Day, Main Street, north from Gold Street, Hartford, September 17, 1879.
COURTESY CONNECTICUT STATE LIBRARY / #PICTURE GROUP 400 HARTFORD COLLECTION 1885-1936, PARADES & PROCESSIONS-RESIDENTS, BOX 4 OF 5

John and Isabella Beecher's home, Forest Street, Nook Farm, circa 1883. COURTESY HARRIET BEECHER STOWE CENTER

RIGHT: The *Hartford Courant* building festooned with patriotic banners (perhaps for Independence Day), 64–68 State Street, circa 1890. The Hartford National Bank is pictured on the left and the National Exchange Bank is on the right. The first floor of the *Courant* building housed commercial establishments. At left is Clapp & Treat Hardware (which later moved to West Hartford) and what appears to be a men's clothing shop. The building was built in 1880 of red brick. COURTESY THE HARTFORD COURANT

BELOW RIGHT: Post Office and Custom House, City Hall Square, Hartford, 1885. COURTESY CONNECTICUT STATE LIBRARY / #PICTURE GROUP 400, HARTFORD COLLECTIONS, 1885-1936, BUILDING-DRUGSTORES, BOX 2 OF 5

OPPOSITE: Hartford looking northeast from the Capitol, 1892. COURTESY CONNECTICUT STATE LIBRARY / #PICTURE GROUP 400, HARTFORD COLLECTION 1885-1936, AERIAL & GENERAL VIEWS, BRIDGES

ABOVE: An elevated view of Hartford looking southwest from the Capitol, 1892. COURTESY CONNECTICUT STATE LIBRARY / #PICTURE GROUP 400, HARTFORD COLLECTION 1885-1936, AERIAL & GENERAL VIEWS, BRIDGES

LEFT: Looking west at Hartford from the Capitol, 1892. COURTESY CONNECTICUT STATE LIBRARY / #PICTURE GROUP 400, HARTFORD COLLECTION 1885-1936, AERIAL & GENERAL VIEWS, BRIDGES

OPPOSITE: A view of crowds on the State Capitol grounds, Hartford, circa late 1800s. COURTESY B. R. BECKWITH COLLECTION

A picturesque view of the Capitol grounds, Hartford. COURTESY CONNECTICUT STATE LIBRARY / #PICTURE GROUP 400, HARTFORD COLLECTION 1885-1936, AERIAL & GENERAL VIEWS, BRIDGES

ABOVE: Asylum Street looking from Main Street, Hartford, late 1800s. COURTESY CONNECTICUT STATE LIBRARY / #PICTURE GROUP 400 HARTFORD COLLECTION 1885-1936, RESTAURANTS-TROLLEYS, BOX 5 OF 5

ABOVE LEFT: This temporary wooden bridge connecting Hartford and East Hartford, opened June 8, 1895. Just six months later it was swept away by floodwaters on December 23, 1895. COURTESY CONNECTICUT STATE LIBRARY / #PICTURE GROUP 400, HARTFORD COLLECTION 1885-1936, AERIAL & GENERAL VIEWS, BRIDGES

LEFT: The State Capitol from Washington Street. COURTESY CONNECTICUT STATE LIBRARY / #PICTURE GROUP 400, HARTFORD COLLECTION 1885-1936, AERIAL & GENERAL VIEWS, BRIDGES

ABOVE: A group of children run a toboggan through the intersection of Linwood and Hart Streets, New Britain. COURTESY PAUL GLAESER COLLECTION / NEW BRITAIN INDUSTRIAL MUSEUM, DIV. OF NEW BRITAIN INSTITUTE / #PAUL GLAESER

ABOVE RIGHT: Talcott Street west of Charles Street, Hartford, 1900. COURTESY CONNECTICUT STATE LIBRARY / #PICTURE GROUP 420 TAYLOR COLLECTIONS, EARLY HARTFORD PHOTOGRAPHS 185-1915, BOX 2

RIGHT: Front Street, north of Talcott Street, Hartford, 1900. COURTESY CONNECTICUT STATE LIBRARY / #PICTURE GROUP 420 TAYLOR COLLECTIONS, EARLY HARTFORD PHOTOGRAPHS 185-1915, BOX 2

Park River from Main Street bridge looking west, Hartford, circa 1900. COURTESY CONNECTICUT STATE LIBRARY / #PICTURE GROUP 420 TAYLOR COLLECTIONS, EARLY HARTFORD PHOTOGRAPHS 185-1915, BOX 1

ABOVE: Main Street in Hartford, 1901. First Church of Christ (Center Church) can be seen in background. COURTESY FRED DOLE

ABOVE RIGHT: Ethel Frances and her mother in front of their house at the corner of Blue Hills Avenue and Albany Avenue, Hartford, 1905. COURTESY TERENCE F. MCNULTY

RIGHT: Main Street from Mulberry Street, Hartford. COURTESY CONNECTICUT STATE LIBRARY / #PICTURE GROUP 400, HARTFORD COLLECTIONS, 1885-1936, BUILDING-DRUGSTORES, BOX 2 OF 5

OPPOSITE: Main Street with view of City Hall, Hartford, circa 1905. COURTESY LIBRARY OF CONGRESS, PRINTS & PHOTOGRAPHS DIVISION, DETROIT PUBLISHING CO., LC-DIG-DET-4A12212

RIGHT: The Connecticut Mutual Life Insurance Company, Hartford, circa 1907.
COURTESY LIBRARY OF CONGRESS, PRINTS & PHOTOGRAPHS DIVISION, DETROIT PUBLISHING CO., LC-DIG-DET-4A13775

ABOVE: Main Street looking south from Hartford Trust to St. John's Church, Hartford, 1905.
COURTESY CONNECTICUT STATE LIBRARY / #RG 064 PICTORIAL ARCHIVES TAYLOR COLLECTIONS PG 420, EARLY HARTFORD PHOTOGRAPHS 185-1915, BOX 1

LEFT: Allyn House, Hartford, circa 1908. COURTESY LIBRARY OF CONGRESS, PRINTS & PHOTOGRAPHS DIVISION, DETROIT PUBLISHING CO.,
LC-DIG-DET-4A22514

LEFT: The First Church of Christ (Center Church), corner of Main and Gold Streets, Hartford, circa 1912. This fourth Meeting House was built of brick from Windsor in 1807. COURTESY CENTER CHURCH, FIRST CHURCH OF CHRIST

OPPOSITE TOP LEFT: Center Church House for the educational and social work of First Church of Christ (Center Church), 60 Gold Street, Hartford, circa 1910. COURTESY CENTER CHURCH, FIRST CHURCH OF CHRIST

OPPOSITE TOP RIGHT: City Hall decorated for Elihu Burritt Day celebration, West Main Street, New Britain, 1910. At age 17 Burritt became an apprentice blacksmith. While working this trade, he taught himself almost 50 foreign languages, earning himself the moniker "the Learned Blacksmith." To further his education, Burritt moved to Massachusetts and studied from the collections of the American Antiquarian Society. It was at this time that he dedicated himself to the peace cause and became the leading pacifist of his age. COURTESY NEW BRITAIN INDUSTRIAL MUSEUM, DIV. OF NEW BRITAIN INSTITUTE

OPPOSITE BOTTOM: Travelers cross the newly completed Bulkeley Bridge over the Connecticut River, Hartford, 1908. COURTESY DONALD JACOBS

ABOVE: Postcard of four men standing in front of the Andover Post Office. COURTESY DONALD JACOBS

ABOVE RIGHT: Downtown view of Hartford, circa 1921. Travelers Tower was the seventh tallest building in the world when it was constructed in 1919. COURTESY CONNECTICUT STATE LIBRARY / #PICTURE GROUP 400, HARTFORD COLLECTION 1885-1936, AERIAL & GENERAL VIEWS, BRIDGES

RIGHT: Corner of Linwood and Hart Streets, New Britain. COURTESY PAUL GLAESER COLLECTION / NEW BRITAIN INDUSTRIAL MUSEUM, DIV. OF NEW BRITAIN INSTITUTE / #PAUL GLAESER COLLECTION

OPPOSITE TOP: Hartford waterfront as seen from the East Hartford side of the Connecticut River shows the Hartford steamboat landing near State Street, circa 1920s. The *City of Springfield* passenger vessel is docked at the wharf. COURTESY RAYMOND LIBRARY COLLECTION

OPPOSITE BOTTOM: Main Street, Rockville. COURTESY DONALD JACOBS

LEFT: The William Herbert Corbin home, 172 Collins Street, Hartford, circa 1930. Corbin served as Connecticut State Tax Commissioner from 1907 until his retirement in 1920. He also played football for Yale College from 1886–1888. COURTESY TESSIE SMINOFF FAMILY

BELOW LEFT: The Clark Building and adjacent shops along the north side of Farmington Avenue, West Hartford Center, 1935. COURTESY NOAH WEBSTER HOUSE AND WEST HARTFORD HISTORICAL SOCIETY

OPPOSITE: Aerial view of Hartford, circa 1927. COURTESY CONNECTICUT STATE LIBRARY / #PICTURE GROUP 400, HARTFORD COLLECTION 1885-1936, AERIAL & GENERAL VIEWS, BRIDGES

LEFT: Postcard of the Church of the Good Shepherd under floodwaters, Hartford, 1936. COURTESY DONALD JACOBS

BELOW: Crowds of people examine floodwater near the First Congregational Church toward the intersection with Main Street on Connecticut Boulevard, East Hartford, March 19, 1936. The Great Connecticut River Flood of 1936 was the highest water level ever recorded in town. COURTESY HISTORICAL SOCIETY OF EAST HARTFORD

OPPOSITE: Overlooking a flooded downtown Hartford, 1936. COURTESY DONALD JACOBS

ABOVE: A flooded downtown street in Hartford with the State Capitol visible in the background, 1936. COURTESY NORA OAKES HOWARD

ABOVE RIGHT: A flood-ravaged Hartford seen from the Travelers Tower, March 1936. Visible are Sheldon Street and the Colt Building. COURTESY CHERYL CORMIER

RIGHT: Downtown Hartford flood scene, 1936. COURTESY LINDSEY FYFE

OPPOSITE: The corner of Oakwood Avenue and New Park Avenue, West Hartford, 1937. COURTESY NOAH WEBSTER HOUSE AND WEST HARTFORD HISTORICAL SOCIETY

CHAPTER TWO

Transportation

Connecticut from the beginning nourished inventors, manufacturers, and retailers who were eager to reach wider markets, a business-minded disposition that required a reliable transportation grid.

The state was fortunate to have a coast between New York and Boston with good harbors for passenger and merchant ships, including the famous New London whalers.

The interior network, however, took longer to develop.

Photos in this chapter show the evolution of the state's transportation infrastructure, from the swampy roadway in West Hartford where a delivery wagon was mired in mud to the pioneering flight center that is now Hartford-Brainard Airport.

Roads in the early years of European settlement often were impassable. Starting in the late eighteenth century, a system of turnpikes began snaking across the state. The first turnpikes were just that—toll roads with revolving gates to allow or block traffic.

But before the advent of the automobile and widespread use of asphalt and concrete, roads were not the reliable way to go. Business owners and other deep-pocket investors banked on canals and railroads.

Connecticut canals were relatively short-lived, but railroads steadily expanded.

Freight and passenger depots were built in just about every community. Some stations, like the passenger depot on Hartford's Asylum Street, were elegant buildings with arched windows and varied textures in brick and stone.

Steamboats offered alternative passage, particularly from Hartford to New York City, and ferryboats such as the *Gen. Spencer* (page 35) were indispensable before sturdy, fireproof bridges traversed the length of the Connecticut River.

In the decades straddling the nineteenth and twentieth centuries, many more connections were made with a 1,000-mile-long maze of electrical railway, the first large-scale mass transit system in most towns. As *Courant* reporter Don Stacom wrote in a 2014 article, "The scope of the system seems almost inconceivable today."

"Small towns from Stafford to Stonington had electric-powered trolleys running down their main streets," Stacom wrote, "and cities such as New Haven and Hartford had sprawling networks with multiple lines linking neighborhoods in every direction."

Also called trams and streetcars, trolleys

evolved from horse-drawn cars, a step up from carriages because rails reduced friction, so horses could go faster and pull more weight. Electrical trolleys replaced horsecars in the late 1880s, and cars replaced trolleys by the late 1930s. A photo on page 43 shows New Britain's last trolley in 1937.

Trolleys connected outlying areas with industrial centers. Cars greatly accelerated the process. As the street grid grew, housing construction followed.

As in many other areas, Connecticut hosted aviation pioneers. Brainard Field was carved out of a 350-acre cow pasture in Hartford's South Meadows. Named for Hartford Mayor Newton C. Brainard, it was dedicated in June 1921. The kickoff ceremony—a monster truck rally of the day—included a seaplane race to Middletown and a contest in which pilots tried to "bomb" targets with sacks of flour.

The airfield's status was boosted in July 1927, when Charles A. Lindbergh stopped first at Brainard on a national victory tour after his solo transatlantic flight.

"Hartford is to be complimented on foreseeing the future of aviation, and breaking the ice, so to speak, by putting in a good airport," Lindbergh said.

OPPOSITE: The Woodland Paper Mill with railroad track siding used for box car pickup, Woodland section of Burnside by upper falls of the Hockanum River, late 1880s. The track crossed Burnside Avenue to connect to the main line of railroad. This was the former site of the Pitkin Gunpowder Works started in 1775 that supplied the Colonial Army during the early years of the American War for Independence. COURTESY HISTORICAL SOCIETY OF EAST HARTFORD

ABOVE: Rocky Hill ferry crossing the Connecticut River. COURTESY DONALD JACOBS

ABOVE RIGHT: The charred remains of the old toll bridge at Hartford shortly after it was destroyed by fire May 17, 1895. The bridge was built in 1818. COURTESY CONNECTICUT STATE LIBRARY / #PICTURE GROUP 400, HARTFORD COLLECTION 1885-1936, AERIAL & GENERAL VIEWS, BRIDGES

RIGHT: Passenger and freight railroad station located northwest of the Main Street underpass, East Hartford, 1890s. This station was one of two in East Hartford. Many in town who worked in Hartford used the railroad to commute before there was trolley service. COURTESY HISTORICAL SOCIETY OF EAST HARTFORD

ABOVE: Passenger depot, Asylum Street, Hartford.
COURTESY CONNECTICUT STATE LIBRARY / #PICTURE GROUP 400, HARTFORD COLLECTION 1885-1936,
AERIAL & GENERAL VIEWS, BRIDGES

LEFT: A postcard of Westbrook Station, Westbrook.
COURTESY CONNECTICUT STATE LIBRARY / #PG800 POSTCARDS, CONNECTICUT ROCKVILLE-WESTPORT BOX 15

ABOVE: J. H. Fish delivery wagon and horse stuck in the mud, Newington Road, West Hartford. The photo was taken by Helen A. Sears to show that the road needed attention. COURTESY NOAH WEBSTER HOUSE AND WEST HARTFORD HISTORICAL SOCIETY

LEFT: The *Gen. Spencer* ferry, East Haddam, 1904. COURTESY CONNECTICUT STATE LIBRARY / #PG800 POSTCARDS, CONNECTICUT DANBURY-GREENWICH BOX 3

ABOVE: Aviation Day, Walnut Hill Park, New Britain, July 2, 1910. New Britain aviator Charles Hamilton is pictured at left, with cigarette, standing next to his Curtiss Pusher aircraft. This was the first public manned flight in New England. Hamilton was famous internationally in his lifetime.
COURTESY NEW BRITAIN INDUSTRIAL MUSEUM, DIV. OF NEW BRITAIN INSTITUTE

LEFT: John F. Preston drives a horse-drawn home-delivery wagon for Preston's Market, Hartford, circa 1910. COURTESY THE PRESTON FAMILY

OPPOSITE: This electric trolley car heads west on Burnside Avenue to connect with Main Street going south, East Hartford, 1905. The advent of the trolley helped make East Hartford one of Hartford's first suburbs. Note the various modes of travel pictured.
COURTESY HISTORICAL SOCIETY OF EAST HARTFORD

RIGHT: Andrew C. Petersen delivers milk for a dairy owned by his cousin, Front Street, Hartford, circa 1914. COURTESY THE PETERSEN FAMILY

BELOW RIGHT: M. J. Burnham Grocery horse-drawn delivery wagon, West Hartford, 1912. COURTESY NOAH WEBSTER HOUSE AND WEST HARTFORD HISTORICAL SOCIETY

BELOW: Electric street car passes under railroad bridge, Main Street, East Hartford, circa 1910. To extend trolley service north on Main Street, the crossing was made by lowering road below the railroad tracks. COURTESY HISTORICAL SOCIETY OF EAST HARTFORD

LEFT: Train conductor in front of the Western Union office at the train depot, New Britain. COURTESY NEW BRITAIN INDUSTRIAL MUSEUM, DIV. OF NEW BRITAIN INSTITUTE

BELOW: Part of the A. C. Petersen Farms delivery fleet, 240 Park Road, West Hartford, 1920s. COURTESY THE PETERSEN FAMILY

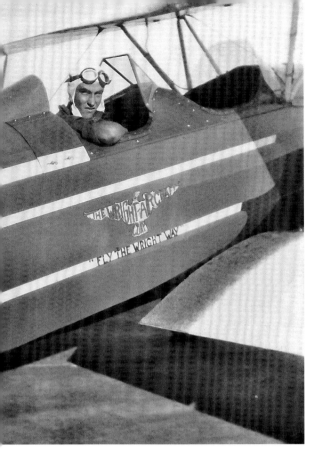

ABOVE: A. C. Petersen milk delivery wagon, West Hartford, 1930s. "Speed" Anderson is the driver. COURTESY THE PETERSEN FAMILY

ABOVE LEFT: Charles Brewer takes flying lessons, Brainard Field, Hartford, summer 1932. COURTESY AL BREWER FAMILY ARCHIVE

LEFT: Delivery wagons line up in front of M. J. Burnham's grocery store, West Hartford. COURTESY NOAH WEBSTER HOUSE AND WEST HARTFORD HISTORICAL SOCIETY

OPPOSITE: The Robert Barnes family in their car in front of the First Church of Windsor parish house, across the street from Broad Street, Windsor, 1920s. Barnes was a druggist in Windsor. COURTESY WINDSOR HISTORICAL SOCIETY, WINDSOR, CT / #2015.1.69

Charles Brewer with his 1932 Chevy at the family farm on High Street, East Hartford, summer 1934. COURTESY AL BREWER FAMILY ARCHIVE

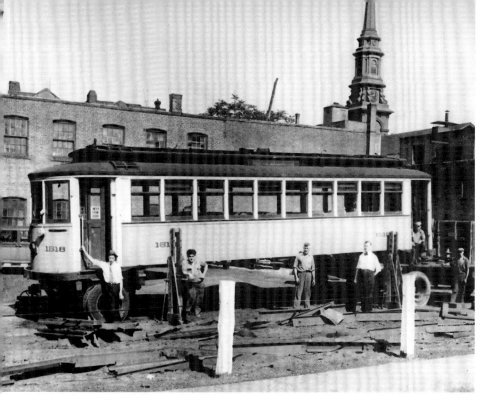

ABOVE: Constable Maurice Kennedy at the scene of an automobile accident on Palisado Avenue in front of First Church, Windsor, 1930s.
COURTESY WINDSOR HISTORICAL SOCIETY, WINDSOR, CT / #2015.1.72

ABOVE LEFT: Connecticut Railway & Lighting Co. trolley, New Britain, 1937. This was the city's last trolley.
COURTESY NEW BRITAIN INDUSTRIAL MUSEUM, DIV. OF NEW BRITAIN INSTITUTE

LEFT: Boys watch as fire engulfs the old trestle that carried trains across the river floodplain between Hartford and East Hartford, North Meadows, November 1936.
COURTESY RAYMOND LIBRARY COLLECTION

CHAPTER THREE

Commerce

The Yankee peddler—contrary to the legend of the con artist hawking wooden nutmegs—was an intrepid character who ventured all along the East Coast and as far west as the Mississippi River on clattering wagons stocked with tin ware, clocks, and other goods.

The world famous Stanley Works in New Britain was founded by Frederick T. Stanley, who got his start selling hardware on horse-and-wagon trips to the back country of North Carolina.

As in many other areas, Connecticut's commercial proprietors pioneered sales of everything from insurance to newspapers.

Insurance today protects health, property, life, and savings, but fear of fire was the initial focus. On April 14, 1794, Sanford & Wadsworth placed an ad in *The Connecticut Courant* for the Hartford Fire Insurance Office, insuring houses, household furniture, goods, wares, and merchandise against fire.

As the economy expanded and the population grew throughout the nineteenth century, insurance companies seized on a demand for all kinds of property protection, including tornado insurance. Insurance company profits built many fortunes in Hartford and its suburbs, funding opulent office buildings (page 53) and mansions on Prospect Avenue.

Newspapers were another reliable money-maker. Many newspapers launched and died through the years, but *The Courant*, founded in 1764 and the oldest continuously published newspaper in the nation, had an able and constant competitor for 159 years.

Rivalry between *The Hartford Times* (page 46) and *The Courant* boiled over during the Civil War, when editors traded charges of cowardice, deceit and anti-Americanism. *The Courant*, a Republican paper opposed to the expansion of slavery, painted *The Times* as a toady to Southern traitors bent on maiming and killing Connecticut's sons. *The Times*, aligned with anti-war, state's rights Democrats, countered by stamping *The Courant* as an abolitionist mouthpiece for a ruinous war. *The Times* closed on October 20, 1976, a victim, some said, to changing reading habits and the nationwide demise of afternoon papers.

Tough times also confronted storefront retailers, and not just in the 1970s when Westfarms and other malls opened. The advent of department stores in the late nineteenth century fostered a common complaint among independent retailers about the loss of personal connections between store owners and customers.

The photos of grocery, drug, and hardware stores here also show the shifting ground in retail as more immigrants set up shop in Hartford and the region. Old Yankee names such as Goodwin (page 46) mixed with Old World names such as DiFabio (opposite photo) and Zinkerman (page 58).

OPPOSITE: Interior of Bonner Market butcher shop, corner of Zion and Bonner Streets, Hartford, circa 1938. From left: Frank A. DiFabio, Vincenzo DiFabio (father), and Anthony F. DiFabio. COURTESY ANTHONY DIFABIO

ABOVE: *Hartford Times* building, Main Street, 1885. COURTESY CONNECTICUT STATE LIBRARY / #PICTURE GROUP 400, HARTFORD COLLECTIONS, 1885-1936, BUILDING-DRUGSTORES, BOX 2 OF 5

OPPOSITE: Four men on the steps in front of Goodwin's Drug Store, 334–336 Main Street, downtown Hartford, circa 1890. COURTESY BARBARA GIRARD

Saloon with patrons in basement of Parsons Theatre, Hartford, circa 1890.

ABOVE: L. H. Bogue General Store included a post office and was a popular meeting place in town, Main Street at the corner of Silver Lane, East Hartford, 1892. The store owners and customers are pictured.
COURTESY HISTORICAL SOCIETY OF EAST HARTFORD

ABOVE LEFT: Albert Gaines stands in front of his harness store, Main Street in the center of town, East Hartford, circa 1890. Note the center opening in the building, which allowed a horse and wagon to pass through to the rear parking area. Pictured are other businesses including a dentist office, a drug store, and the weekly *Gazette* which is still a weekly town newspaper today.
COURTESY HISTORICAL SOCIETY OF EAST HARTFORD

LEFT: Wyman J. May Hardware Store, Ford Street near Pearl Street, Hartford. COURTESY CONNECTICUT STATE LIBRARY / #PICTURE GROUP 400, HARTFORD COLLECTIONS, 1885-1936, BUILDING-DRUGSTORES, BOX 2 OF 5

Geo. F. Loeffler Drugstore, 243 Main Street, Hartford, circa 1897. H. Howard Wallace is on the right. COURTESY CONNECTICUT STATE LIBRARY / #PICTURE GROUP 400, HARTFORD COLLECTIONS, 1885-1936, BUILDING-DRUGSTORES, BOX 2 OF 5

The back room of Geo. F. Loeffler Drugstore, 243 Main Street, Hartford, circa 1897. H. Howard Wallace is on the right. COURTESY CONNECTICUT STATE LIBRARY / #PICTURE GROUP 400, HARTFORD COLLECTIONS, 1885-1936, BUILDING-DRUGSTORES, BOX 2 OF 5

LEFT: The Aetna and Charter Oak Insurance buildings, Main Street, Hartford. COURTESY CONNECTICUT STATE LIBRARY / #PICTURE GROUP 400, HARTFORD COLLECTION 1885-1936, AERIAL & GENERAL VIEWS, BRIDGES

BELOW LEFT: Lawrence Mullaley store, 194 Broad Street, Windsor, early 1900s. Mullaley sold groceries, provisions, and general merchandise. COURTESY WINDSOR HISTORICAL SOCIETY, WINDSOR, CT / #2015.1.127

OPPOSITE: The W. E. Truesdell & Company store, Tolland Street in the Burnside section of East Hartford, late 1800s. The proprietors are pictured standing in front of the store. The store sold household goods and farm items, such as seeds. COURTESY RAYMOND LIBRARY COLLECTION

ABOVE: Cheney Building, 400 Main Street, Hartford.
COURTESY CONNECTICUT STATE LIBRARY / #PICTURE GROUP 400, HARTFORD COLLECTION 1885-1936, AERIAL & GENERAL VIEWS, BRIDGES

RIGHT: Emil Rosenthal and family stand in front of their grocery store, 150 Burnside Avenue, East Hartford, 1900. COURTESY HISTORICAL SOCIETY OF EAST HARTFORD

OPPOSITE: Interior of the Charles Ende Barber Shop, Poquonock, circa 1900. Note the owner's reflection in the mirror.
COURTESY DAVID AND MARY LOU PETERS AND EDWARD ENDEE, WINDSOR HISTORICAL SOCIETY COLLECTIONS 2007.14.1

RIGHT: Bidwell Hardware store, 1293 Main Street, Hartford, circa 1905. Owner Frederick C. Bidwell is pictured. COURTESY BRUCE E. BIDWELL

BELOW: Businesses at the foot of Pearl Street looking from the north corner of Ford Street, Hartford, circa 1905. COURTESY CONNECTICUT STATE LIBRARY / #PICTURE GROUP 420 TAYLOR COLLECTIONS, EARLY HARTFORD PHOTOGRAPHS 1895-1915, BOX 2

ABOVE: Shoor Bro's furniture store, Hartford, 1908. The business was started by Philip and Jacob Shoor in 1908. Abraham Shoor joined the company the day after Philip left. Over time the business moved from Sigourney House (pictured) to Main Street and then to Trumbull Street. The brothers sold the business in 1928. COURTESY JEWISH HISTORICAL SOCIETY OF GREATER HARTFORD

ABOVE LEFT: Marwick Drugstore Company, Main and Asylum Streets, Hartford, 1908. Charles Allen and H. Howard Wallace are pictured.
COURTESY CONNECTICUT STATE LIBRARY / #PICTURE GROUP 400, HARTFORD COLLECTIONS, 1885-1936, BUILDING-DRUGSTORES, BOX 2 OF 5

LEFT: W. G. Wrisley & Sons livery stable, Central Street, Windsor, 1910. Mack, Walter, and George Wrisley are pictured standing on the steps.
COURTESY WINDSOR HISTORICAL SOCIETY, WINDSOR, CT / #2011.1.7

I. Zinkerman & Sons Grocery Store, corner of Broad and Madison Streets, Hartford, November 10, 1929. Pictured from left are Isadore Zinkerman (owner), and sons Howard and Frank. COURTESY THE ZINKERMAN FAMILY

ABOVE: Second Anniversary of the Grand opening of The Windsor Trust and Safe Deposit Company Bank, Windsor, February 16, 1916. Each student in attendance was given a ruler and an orange. COURTESY WINDSOR HISTORICAL SOCIETY, WINDSOR, CT / #2008.1.18

ABOVE LEFT: A girl in Mr. Judd's Drugstore, West Hartford Center, circa 1915. COURTESY NOAH WEBSTER HOUSE AND WEST HARTFORD HISTORICAL SOCIETY

LEFT: The casket display room at the Newkirk & Whitney Funeral Home, 776 Farmington Avenue, West Hartford, 1931. COURTESY LISA (CHRISTENSEN) PETERSEN

ABOVE: These businesses at Main and Governor Streets are patriotically decorated for an upcoming parade, East Hartford, 1933. The repeal of prohibition saw the return of taverns and package stores to Main Streets here and across the country. COURTESY RAYMOND LIBRARY COLLECTION

OPPOSITE: Burnham's Grocery Store, West Hartford, circa 1930. COURTESY NOAH WEBSTER HOUSE AND WEST HARTFORD HISTORICAL SOCIETY

CHAPTER FOUR

Agriculture and Industry

The people of Connecticut are inventors and makers and have been since the first Colonists arrived. Made-in-Connecticut items includes guns, airplane engines, submarines, helicopters, tools, hardware, typewriters, mechanical banks, brass shells, blenders, bicycles, Wiffle balls, and Pez candy dispensers.

Mark Twain, a keen observer and longtime Hartford resident, described the state's inventive, industrious character through the protagonist of *A Connecticut Yankee in King Arthur's Court.*

"I am an American. I was born and reared in Hartford, in the State of Connecticut—anyway, just over the river, in the country. So I am a Yankee of the Yankees—and practical; yes, and nearly barren of sentiment, I suppose—or poetry, in other words. My father was a blacksmith, my uncle was a horse doctor, and I was both, along at first. Then I went over to the great arms factory and learned my real trade; learned all there was to it; learned to make everything: guns, revolvers, cannon, boilers, engines, all sorts of labor-saving machinery. Why, I could make anything a body wanted—anything in the world,

it didn't make any difference what; and if there wasn't any quick new-fangled way to make a thing, I could invent one—and do it as easy as rolling off a log."

The "great arms factory" was, of course, Colt's Patent Firearms Manufacturing Co. World famous guns made in Samuel Colt's onion-domed factory included the Single Action Army Model 1873, better known as "the gun that won the West;" the first successful gas-powered machine gun to enter service, the Colt-Browning M1895; and the .45-caliber Colt 1911 semi-automatic pistol, for many years the official sidearm of the United States Army.

Hartford also became known as "the bicycle capital of the world" because of Albert Pope, who studied how bicycles were made in Europe and returned to Hartford to make his own, beginning with the Columbia High Wheeler in 1878. Pope later added automobiles to the Pope Manufacturing Co., focusing on electric cars.

Francis Pratt and Amos Whitney, apprentice machinists for Colt, founded their own eponymous company in Hartford in 1860, engineering and developing machine tools and gauges with a focus on precision.

In 1925, Frederick B. Rentschler carried the company name to East Hartford, where he started an airplane engine company.

Industry eclipsed agriculture in the Greater Hartford area, but one crop won world fame—Connecticut shade tobacco, the preferred wrapper for fine cigars.

Brought to Connecticut from the island of Sumatra at the end of the nineteenth century, Connecticut shade's superior qualities—unduplicated in other tobacco-growing countries—come from an unusual combination of heat, high moisture, and the light, well-drained soil of the Connecticut River valley.

Many state natives can tell stories of working in the tobacco fields and sheds in summers gone by.

Tobacco farm owners also hired African American high school and college students from the South for summer work. Before they were famous, the Rev. Martin Luther King Jr., United States Supreme Court Justice Thurgood Marshall, and tennis star Arthur Ashe all worked in the state's tobacco fields.

OPPOSITE: Workers process dried shade tobacco in a tobacco shed, Windsor. Dried leaves were taken off the stems, inspected, sorted by size, and packed in wooden boxes for storage. COURTESY WINDSOR HISTORICAL SOCIETY, WINDSOR, CT / #2012.1.3

RIGHT: New England Granite Works, formerly Batterson, Canfield & Co., 650 Main Street, Hartford, circa 1875.
COURTESY HARRIET BEECHER STOWE CENTER / #NO. 1

Pratt & Whitney Company workers standing on the bridge they built on what is now Flower Street, Hartford, 1875. COURTESY PRATT & WHITNEY MEASUREMENT SYSTEMS

ABOVE: The M. J. Cox Grist Mill on Pewter Pot Brook, Main Street, Hockanum area of East Hartford, 1888. This grist mill serviced local farmers who brought their grain to be ground. COURTESY HISTORICAL SOCIETY OF EAST HARTFORD

ABOVE RIGHT: Workers at the Spencer Machine Screw Works, Windsor, 1880s. Spencer was famous for a repeating rifle used during the Civil War. In 1883 Spencer set up a factory in Windsor to produce repeating shotguns and later turned to making machine tool equipment. COURTESY WINDSOR HISTORICAL SOCIETY, WINDSOR, CT / #2011.1.56

RIGHT: Pratt & Whitney Company workers, Hartford, 1886. Identified in the front row: Francis Pratt (sixth from the left), Amos Whitney (seventh from the left). COURTESY PRATT & WHITNEY MEASUREMENT SYSTEMS

Employees of Colt's Patent Fire Arms Manufacturing Company in front of the company Armory, Hartford. COURTESY CONNECTICUT STATE LIBRARY / #PG 460 COLT'S PATENT FIRE ARMS MANUFACTURING COMPANY COLLECTION, PORTRAITS, BOX 2

ABOVE: Workers size shade-grown tobacco, East Hartford, circa 1900. COURTESY RAYMOND LIBRARY COLLECTION

ABOVE RIGHT: Workers hang shade tobacco to dry in a tobacco shed, Windsor. Small fires were used to help dry the tobacco while temperature and humidity was regulated by adjusting the vertical side slates of the shed. The leaves hung in the shed for approximately eight weeks. After the leaves were dry, they were taken off the stems, sorted by size and packed in wooden boxes for storage. COURTESY WINDSOR HISTORICAL SOCIETY, WINDSOR, CT / #1954.2.8.70

RIGHT: Leonard family members work alongside hired help to harvest broadleaf tobacco for drying, Forest Street, East Hartford, circa 1900. COURTESY RAYMOND LIBRARY COLLECTION

Goodwin Brothers Pottery employees, West Hartford. COURTESY NOAH WEBSTER HOUSE AND WEST HARTFORD HISTORICAL SOCIETY

ABOVE: Norman Howard Brewer on a parade float in front of the Brewer family homestead in the Hockanum area on High Street, East Hartford, circa 1910. The float was likely prepared for an agricultural fair or local parade. Norman became a wealthy tobacco farmer, wholesale tobacco dealer, and award-winning corn grower. He also served on the Connecticut State Board of Agriculture and with the Connecticut Agricultural Experiment Station. COURTESY HISTORICAL SOCIETY OF EAST HARTFORD

ABOVE LEFT: Milkmen for the Vine Hill Dairy, West Hartford. COURTESY NOAH WEBSTER HOUSE AND WEST HARTFORD HISTORICAL SOCIETY

LEFT: Newsboys, Hartford, March 1909. Some of the boys pictured were as young as seven and eight years old. COURTESY LIBRARY OF CONGRESS, PRINTS & PHOTOGRAPHS DIVISION, LC-DIG-NCLC-03246

OPPOSITE: Women employees of the Goodwin Pottery company, West Hartford. The women painted and decorated the flower pots. COURTESY NOAH WEBSTER HOUSE AND WEST HARTFORD HISTORICAL SOCIETY

Women inspect Colt 45 automatic pistol parts at Colt's Patent Fire Arms Plant, Hartford, circa 1915. COURTESY LIBRARY OF CONGRESS, PRINTS & PHOTOGRAPHS DIVISION, LC-DIG-PPMSCA-55676

ABOVE: George H. Long with his horse, Bay, on his tobacco farm, School Street, East Hartford, circa 1915. COURTESY ROBERTA L. ROY

ABOVE LEFT: Anders Christensen farm market delivery truck loaded with produce, Meadow Road, Wilson area of Windsor, 1916. COURTESY CHRISTENSEN FAMILY

LEFT: Mack Brickyard, Windsor, circa 1916. Identified are Floyd Niles (fourth from left), Fred Cooper (right front holding brick). COURTESY WINDSOR HISTORICAL SOCIETY, WINDSOR, CT / #2011.1.18

RIGHT: Construction at Colt's Patent Fire Arms Company's North Armory, Hartford, 1916.
COURTESY CONNECTICUT STATE LIBRARY / #PICTURE GROUP 400, HARTFORD COLLECTION, 1885-1936, FIRES & EXPLOSIVES-MONUMENTS & STATUES, BOX 3 OF 5

BELOW RIGHT: A truckload of child tobacco workers leave Post Office Square in Hartford for American Sumatra Tobacco Farm in South Windsor, August 1917. The workers would leave for work at 6:00 a.m. and return about 7:00 p.m. COURTESY LIBRARY OF CONGRESS, PRINTS & PHOTOGRAPHS DIVISION, LC-DIG-NCLC-00724

OPPOSITE: Harvesting carrots on the Christensen farm, Meadow Road, Wilson area of Windsor, 1916.
COURTESY CHRISTENSEN FAMILY

ABOVE: George H. Long delivers heating oil to his Hartford customers, 1921. COURTESY ROBERTA L. ROY

LEFT: Workers pasteurize and bottle milk at the A. C. Petersen Farms Dairy, 240 Park Road, West Hartford, circa 1923. Identified are Alfred Kristensen and Peter Ottowitz. COURTESY THE PETERSEN FAMILY

OPPOSITE: H. B. Francis Electric workers in front of a company truck advertising payment plans for electrical services, Southington, circa 1924. COURTESY DONALD JACOBS

LEFT: Kenneson Safety Ladder Company owner Ralph Robert Kenneson (standing) and an employee at the company's display at a Hartford trade show held at the State Armory, circa 1925. COURTESY GORDON W. KENNESON

BELOW LEFT: New Park Brickyard employees, West Hartford, 1928. COURTESY NOAH WEBSTER HOUSE AND WEST HARTFORD HISTORICAL SOCIETY

OPPOSITE: Telephone operators inside Burnham's General Store, West Hartford, circa 1925. COURTESY NOAH WEBSTER HOUSE AND WEST HARTFORD HISTORICAL SOCIETY

ABOVE: Stoddard siblings with one of the cows on the family dairy farm, Chapman Street, Newington, Hartford County, circa 1935. From left: Donna Stoddard (Tilley), Marilyn Stoddard (Shieber), K. Elliott Stoddard. COURTESY MARILYN (SHIEBER) SULLIVAN

ABOVE RIGHT: Employees of the payroll department of Corbin Manufacturing, New Britain, late 1920s. From left: Frank C. Johnson, Marion Conrad, Teresa DeZenzo, unidentified. COURTESY NEW BRITAIN INDUSTRIAL MUSEUM, DIV. OF NEW BRITAIN INSTITUTE

RIGHT: Colt's Patent Firearms Manufacturing Company Electrical Division employees, Hartford, July 10, 1935. Front row, from left: ___ Stahl, A. H. Sopes, L. H. McClure, P. L. Asbury, B. Greenspon, E. M. Donofrio, L. White, J. Foley, H. Kearrey, B. F. Smith, E. L. Randle. Middle row: E. Whiton, F. Popowics, K. E. Roberts, H. B. Cole. Back row: D. G. Phelps, A. L. Ulrich, J. Sacks, G. MacMannus, G. A. Saylor, S. A. Beaumont, G. Mason, B. Cotter, N. B. Osborn, C. J. Casey, J. Yates, N. Stark, G. Stout, S. M. Stone, A. B. Fink, F. Gamer, L. M. Pond. COURTESY CONNECTICUT STATE LIBRARY / #PG 460 COLT'S PATIENT FIRE AMS MANUFACTURING COMPANY COLLECTION, PORTRAITS, BOX 2

OPPOSITE: Pratt and Whitney apprenticeship training, Hartford, circa 1935. Victor G. Muzzulin Jr. is pictured second from left. COURTESY VICTOR MUZZULIN FAMILY

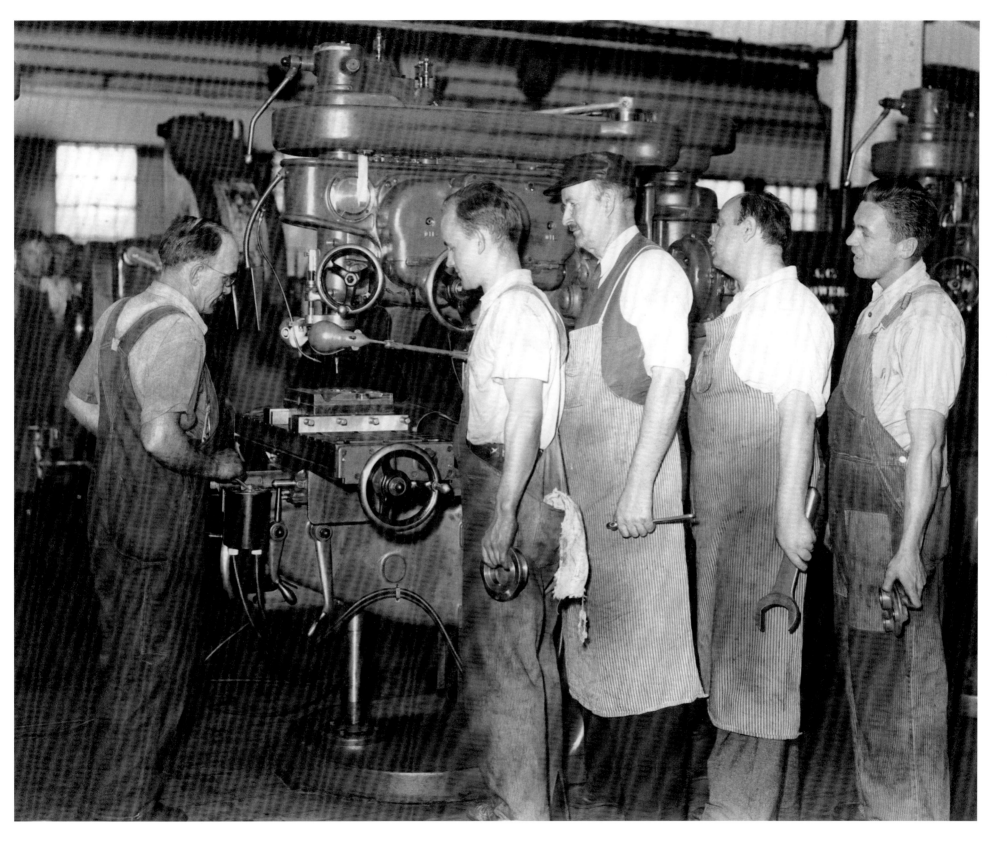

Employees in a sheet metal workshop, 599 Front Street, Hartford, May 21, 1937. From left: Max Landerman, Jim Rudolph, John Cardillo, Manuel Libin. COURTESY SHELLY B. LANDERMAN COLLECTION

LEFT: Selden Brewer drives a truck loaded with salvaged tobacco from a tobacco shed destroyed by the hurricane of 1938. The Vincent Brewer tobacco farm was located on High Street in East Hartford. COURTESY AL BREWER FAMILY ARCHIVE

BELOW: The 91st birthday celebration for Joseph Millard Merrow, owner of Merrow Machine, at the home of Clayton R. Burt on Hunter Drive, West Hartford, June 26, 1939. Merrow designed the overlock sewing machine for crocheting and was a founder of Hartford County Manufacturer's Association. In attendance were manufacturers, inventors, and political leaders of Hartford County and included Graham H. Anthony, Newton C. Brainard, Clayton R. Burt, Charles L. Campbell, H. Bissell Carey, Howell Cheney, Dexter D. Coffin, Frederick U. Conrad, Charles B. Cook, John R. Cook, Sidney E. Cornelius, Samuel Ferguson, Philip B. Gale, James L. Goodwin, Ralph G. Kenneson, Mitchell S. Little, George A. Long, Charles D. Rice, Lucius Rossiter, Robert H. Schutz, Samuel M. Stone, Charles L. Taylor, James A. Taylor, Charles L. Tolles, Samuel P. Williams, Eugene E. Wilson. COURTESY GORDON W. KENNESON

CHAPTER FIVE

Schools and Education

Soon after building their first crude dwellings by the Connecticut River, Hartford settlers established a college preparatory school, supported in part by public funds.

The first classes in 1638 likely were held in city founder Thomas Hooker's home. Little else is known about the early years of what would become Hartford Public High School, but the priority of founding a classical school when other needs were so pressing says much about where Connecticut's Puritan ancestors had been and where they were headed.

They were determined that their children would be able to at least read the Bible. In 1650, Connecticut followed Massachusetts in establishing compulsory education laws. Literacy was fed and maintained by pious leaders who saw idleness and ignorance as the devil's doorways.

Because of their tightly organized settlements, New Englanders were better able to foster schools than their Southern counterparts, who tended to disperse. A study of seventeenth century documents showed that 95 percent contained signatures, as opposed to marks, compared with a literacy rate in Virginia of 54 to 60 percent.

Connecticut colonists read newspapers and other publications. In 1776, they read Thomas Paine's "Common Sense." Is it any wonder that Connecticut men were among the first to answer the alarm at Lexington and Concord? John Adams said the Revolution started well before the first shots were fired—"in the minds and hearts of the people."

"The real revolution had been essentially a matter of popular education," historian Lawrence A. Cremin wrote in *Traditions of American Education*, (Basic Books, Inc., 1977).

Connecticut was home to education pioneers known worldwide, including Elihu Burritt, the "Learned Blacksmith" of New Britain, a largely self-educated speaker, author and peace advocate who could read 50 languages.

Another nineteenth century activist, Hartford native Henry Barnard, pressed for a free secondary school in Hartford that would be "cheap enough for the poorest and good enough for the richest." Richard P. Smith, Hartford Public Class of 1932, remembered that many wealthy Hartford families sent their children to Hartford Public because the education was just as good as what private schools offered. In fact, many families from Avon and other suburbs had their children boarded in the city so they could attend the school.

The high school moved several times. Its most magnificent iteration was the Victorian beauty on Hopkins Street (page 86). The school was divided according to commercial, manual arts, and college preparatory curricula. It was demolished in the early 1960s to make way for I-84, and a new school was built on Forest Street.

College choices in the state included Storrs Agricultural College (pages 87–89), now the University of Connecticut. Established in 1881 as a two-year institution, the college focused on practical education in farming. Thirteen students attended the first term. The annual cost was $25.

State Normal School was established in New Britain in 1849 (which became the Teachers College of Connecticut and then CCSU). The Normal School (Teacher's College) in New Britain was the first in the state (1850) and the only one founded in Hartford County. It remained the only Normal School in Connecticut for 37 years. Additional Normal Schools followed later in the nineteenth century—in Willimantic (1887) and New Haven (1893), and a fourth in Danbury (1903).

OPPOSITE: Cromwell High School under construction, West Street, Cromwell, August 9, 1911. The building is now used as the town hall.
COURTESY DONALD JACOBS

ABOVE: Graduating class of West Middle School, 44 Niles Street, Hartford, April 28, 1888.
COURTESY HARRIET BEECHER STOWE CENTER

ABOVE RIGHT: Northend School students, New Britain, October 1879. COURTESY NEW BRITAIN INDUSTRIAL MUSEUM, DIV. OF NEW BRITAIN INSTITUTE

RIGHT: Hartford High School, Hopkins Street, 1885. COURTESY CONNECTICUT STATE LIBRARY / #PICTURE GROUP 400 HARTFORD COLLECTION 1885-1936, RESTAURANTS-TROLLEYS, BOX 5 OF 5

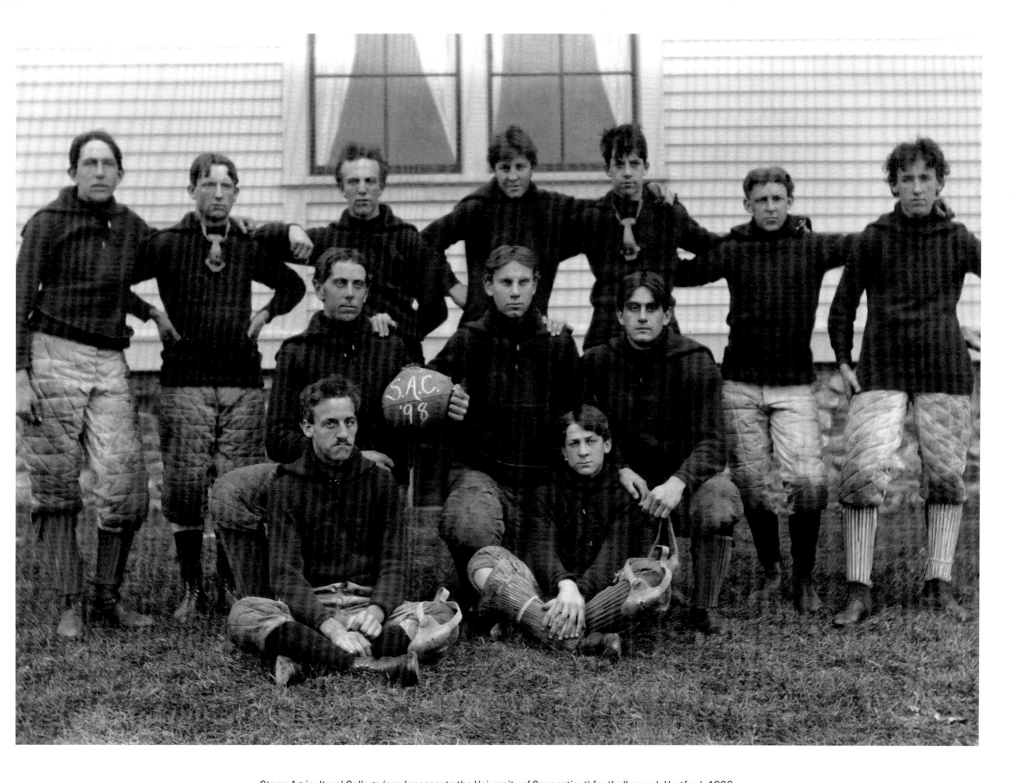

Storrs Agricultural College (predecessor to the University of Connecticut) football squad, Hartford, 1898.

Elevated view of Storrs Agricultural College, Hartford, late 1800s. The school was the predecessor to the University of Connecticut.

COURTESY CONNECTICUT STATE LIBRARY / #PICTURE GROUP 200, CONNECTICUT STATE GOVERNMENT, INSTITUTIONS AND PARKS, 1878-1973 GOVERNMENT BUILDINGS, STATE PARKS & OFFICIALS, BOX 1 OF 3

ABOVE: Storrs Agricultural College Cadet band members, Hartford, late 1800s. Storrs Agricultural College was the predecessor to the University of Connecticut. COURTESY CONNECTICUT STATE LIBRARY / #PICTURE GROUP 200, CONNECTICUT STATE GOVERNMENT, INSTITUTIONS AND PARKS, 1878-1973 GOVERNMENT BUILDINGS, STATE PARKS & OFFICIALS, BOX 1 OF 3

LEFT: Hayden Station School students, Palisado Avenue, Windsor, 1902. COURTESY WINDSOR HISTORICAL SOCIETY, WINDSOR, CT / #1995.59.1.2

LEFT: Students in front of Whiting Lane School, formerly called East School, West Hartford, circa 1905.
COURTESY NOAH WEBSTER HOUSE AND WEST HARTFORD HISTORICAL SOCIETY

BELOW LEFT: West Hartford School orchestra, circa 1907.
COURTESY NOAH WEBSTER HOUSE AND WEST HARTFORD HISTORICAL SOCIETY

OPPOSITE: Students and teachers in front of East Hartford High School, Main and Chapman Streets, East Hartford, early 1900s. This school was destroyed by fire in 1915 and replaced with a new high school in 1917.
COURTESY HISTORICAL SOCIETY OF EAST HARTFORD

ABOVE: West Hartford High School graduating class of 1907. From left: Ed Dissell, Elmer Blackman, Agnes Merriam, Phil Day.
COURTESY NOAH WEBSTER HOUSE AND WEST HARTFORD HISTORICAL SOCIETY

ABOVE RIGHT: Postcard of Trinity College, Hartford.
COURTESY CONNECTICUT STATE LIBRARY / #PG800 POSTCARDS, CONNECTICUT HARTFORD-KILLINGWORTH BOX 6

RIGHT: West Hartford High School baseball team, circa 1907.
COURTESY NOAH WEBSTER HOUSE AND WEST HARTFORD HISTORICAL SOCIETY

Windsor High School (Roger Ludlow School) graduating class of 1911. Front row, from left: Ruth Hayden, Margaret Stinson, Grace Knapp, Anna Barnes. Second row: Leonora Carter, Mildred Shepherd, Henrietta Schrader. Back row (boys): John O'Brien, Frank Snelgrove, Leon Barnes, Raymond Bond, Frederic Nelson, Winthrop Nelson, Oliver M. Hayden. COURTESY WINDSOR HISTORICAL SOCIETY, WINDSOR, CT / #1982.8.2

ABOVE: West Hartford High School girls basketball team, 1911–1912. Miss Louise Day (Duffy) was the teacher. COURTESY NOAH WEBSTER HOUSE AND WEST HARTFORD HISTORICAL SOCIETY

ABOVE RIGHT: Roger Ludlow High School girls basketball team, Windsor, 1921. Front row: Harriet Lang, Lillian Einsiedel, Florence Perry. Back row: Bessie Chamberlain, Mildred Wilbraham, Ruth Reeves, Coach Katherine Judd. The team played against teams in the Farmington Valley League. COURTESY WINDSOR HISTORICAL SOCIETY, WINDSOR, CT / #1954.2.8.100

RIGHT: West Hartford High School graduating class of 1911. Front row: Charlotte Sears, Marion Thorpe, Leroy Watkins, Jennie Christensen, Ruth Sears. Back row: Ethel Codwell, Rhea Carroll, Orson Lata, Bertha Hatch, Ruby Selden, Myrtle Brigham. COURTESY NOAH WEBSTER HOUSE AND WEST HARTFORD HISTORICAL SOCIETY

ABOVE: H. Sidney Hayden Grammar School class of 1927, Windsor.
COURTESY WINDSOR HISTORICAL SOCIETY, WINDSOR, CT / #1998.13.1

LEFT: John Fitch High School baseball team, Bloomfield Avenue, Windsor, 1931. Front row: Clifford Clark, Stuart Waterhouse, Albert Yuskevich, Joseph Mazel. Back row: Charles Noreaker (manager), Adelbert Coe, John Uzdarwin, James Nass, Stanley Peteroski, Charles Buckavich, Willet Clyne, John Powers (coach).
COURTESY WINDSOR HISTORICAL SOCIETY, WINDSOR, CT / #1985.11

RIGHT: Students of Elm Grove School, Windsor, 1932. Front row, from left: Richard Goodrich, Albina Simmons, Douglas Bensenhaver, Dorothy Demay, Leonard Noland, Anna Bakervich, Charles Trisdale. Middle row: Anna Walton, Arthur Bensenhaver, Leon Nolan, Edward Padigenus, Joseph Nolan, Evelyn Milky. Back row: William Milky, Edward Darcy, Priscilla Huntington, Mildred Nolan, Herbert Nolan, Richard Clark.
COURTESY WINDSOR HISTORICAL SOCIETY, WINDSOR, CT / #2018.1.288

BELOW: The graduating class of St. Mary's School, New Britain, 1932. Mortimer Nelson Judd is in the front row, third from the right.
COURTESY NEW BRITAIN INDUSTRIAL MUSEUM, DIV. OF NEW BRITAIN INSTITUTE

ABOVE: Hartford High School graduation ceremonies, 1934. Phyllis Elizabeth Blake is pictured third row, center. COURTESY GORDON W. KENNESON

LEFT: John Fitch High School champion soccer team, Bloomfield Avenue, Windsor, 1938. Front row, from left: Raymond Donahue, Robert T. Silliman, John Kotcha, William King, Sylvester "Sonny" Peters (captain), Douglas Althen, Charles "Iggy" Kosiorek, Stephen Slaker, Victor Grakowski. Second row: John Lukstas, Charles Witkowski, R. Jones, R. "Butler" Schaeffer, Robert Dawes, Thomas Fusco, Gerard Wilson. Back row: Coach Theodore "Ted" Wilson, Manager Albert Gilman. COURTESY WINDSOR HISTORICAL SOCIETY, WINDSOR, CT / #1993.94.3

CHAPTER SIX

Public Service

Police service in 1914 East Hartford was lonely and laborious.

Officers were on foot, with no means to call for help. The department would not get its first patrol car until 1929.

"Drunken or subdued prisoners had to be carried to the lockup, either on the back of the arresting officer, in a wheel barrow, or in a wagon if one was available," according to a history on the department website.

The history of public service in Connecticut follows a pattern—a need is shown; community leaders form a responsive organization; and leaders and taxpayers figure out how to pay for the expanding organization as needs grow.

The Hartford Fire Department, for instance, was formed after the roof of the wooden statehouse caught fire. In 1785, the town council authorized purchase of a hand-operated pumper that firefighters pulled with ropes and the beginning of a public water system—cisterns around the statehouse.

By 1840, the department had 500 volunteers who managed seven engine companies, one hose company and one hook-and-ladder company. The first steam engine was bought in 1861.

The 1864 fire at the Colt Firearms factory that resulted in one death and $1.5 million in damage prompted the city to consider a paid department, and on October 1 the common council authorized one. The ordinance went into effect December 1, 1864.

In 1867, the city purchased and installed a 9,000-pound fire bell in a tower behind the Alert Hose Co. at 43 Pearl Street. Including installation, the bell cost $9,860. It was first put to use in October for a fire at the steamboat storehouse. It also rang a single note at noon and 6 p.m. daily.

Used for 37 years, the bell was operated electrically and connected to 170 fireboxes throughout the city by 50 miles of wire. It is now on the grounds of the Connecticut Historical Society on Elizabeth Street.

Connecticut is called the Provision State and the Arsenal of Democracy for good reason. State workers have produced a staggering volume and variety of war material since cannons for the Revolutionary War were cast in the iron-rich Northwest Hills.

The state also has sent more than its share of natives into combat zones. US entry into World War I spurred patriotic fervor and soaring speeches about the nation's essential part in squashing "the Hun." At a rally outside Hartford city hall on April 7, 1917, Mayor Frank A. Hagarty evoked Connecticut Yankees' response to earlier alarms. Hagarty sought to assure the nation's leaders "that the spirit of loyalty, which filled the breasts of Hartford's people in 1776 and 1861, animate us in 1917."

Connecticut soldiers arrived in Europe early in 1918, among the first American troops to take their place on the jagged front. They were concentrated in the United States Army's 102nd Infantry Regiment of the 26th (Yankee) Division, which comprised men from all New England states. They saw heavy fighting.

Of the 67,000 Connecticut residents who served in the war, about 1,100 died.

OPPOSITE: Connecticut Governor George L. Lilley's funeral procession, Hartford, April 1909. COURTESY DONALD JACOBS

ABOVE: The Governor's Foot Guard on Field Day, Hartford, 1882.
COURTESY CONNECTICUT STATE LIBRARY / #PICTURE GROUP 200, CONNECTICUT STATE GOVERNMENT,
INSTITUTIONS AND PARKS, 1878-1973 GOVERNMENT BUILDINGS, STATE PARKS & OFFICIALS, BOX 1 OF 3

RIGHT: Connecticut Supreme Court Judges, Hartford, circa 1869. From left: Justice
Elisha Carpenter, Chief Justice Joel Hinman, Justice Thomas B. Butler, Justice John
D. Park. COURTESY CONNECTICUT STATE LIBRARY / #PICTURE GROUP 560 CONNECTICUT GROUP PORTRAITS, 1864-1950,
BOX 1 OF 1

OPPOSITE: Republican rally for presidential candidate James G. Blaine held in front
of the "Old State House," Hartford, 1884. COURTESY CONNECTICUT STATE LIBRARY /
#PICTURE GROUP 400 HARTFORD COLLECTION 1885-1936, PARADES & PROCESSIONS-RESIDENTS, BOX 4 OF 5

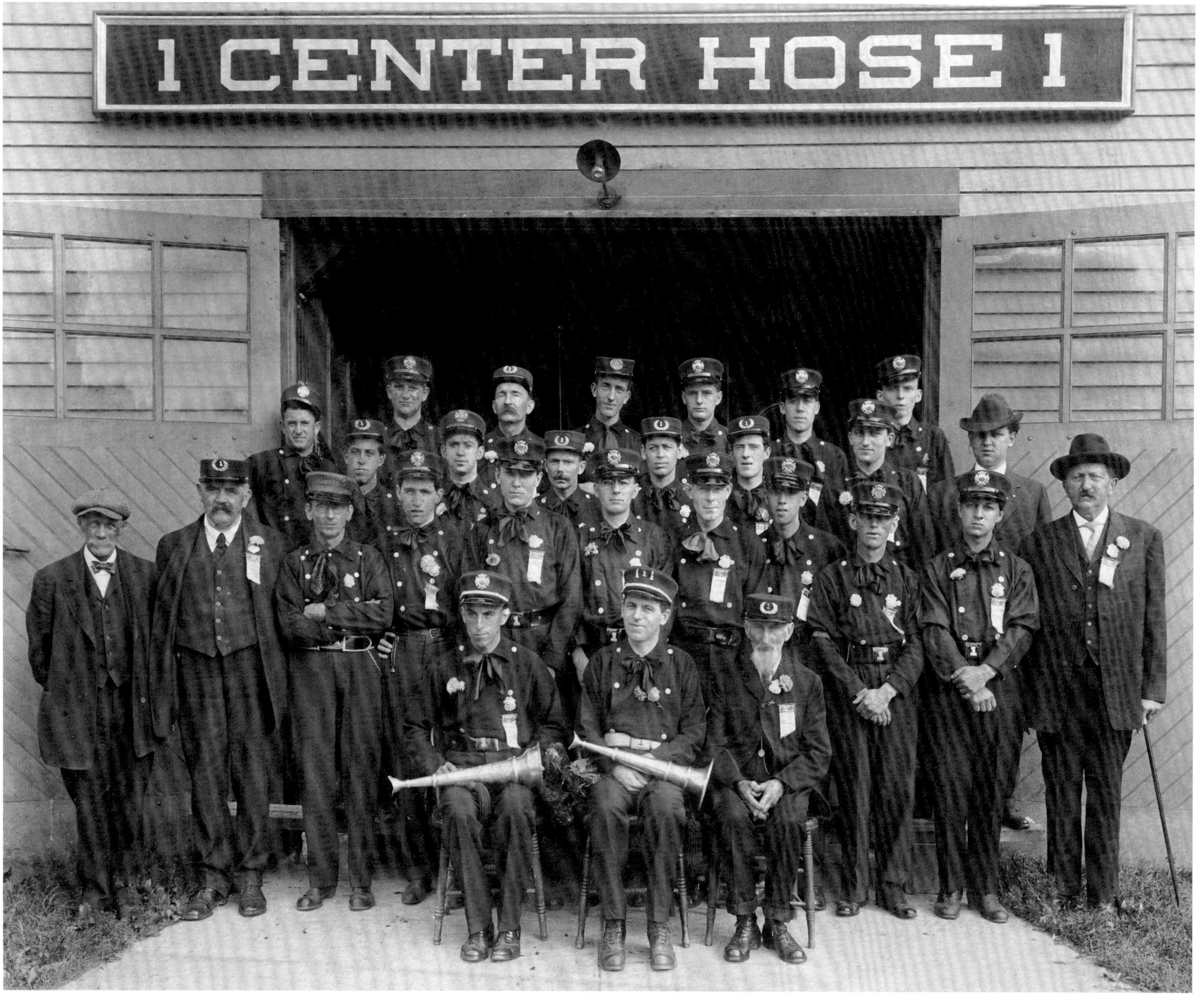
1 CENTER HOSE 1

LEFT: City Hall and Post Office, Hartford, 1900. The Post Office was torn down in 1934. COURTESY CONNECTICUT STATE LIBRARY / #PICTURE GROUP 400, HARTFORD COLLECTIONS, 1885-1936, BUILDING-DRUGSTORES, BOX 2 OF 5

BELOW LEFT: Christian Trudell, New Britain.
COURTESY NEW BRITAIN INDUSTRIAL MUSEUM, DIV. OF NEW BRITAIN INSTITUTE

BELOW RIGHT: Hartford policeman Patrick Doran, circa 1900.
COURTESY JOSEPH DORAN

OPPOSITE: The volunteer firemen of Center Hose Company 1, Bissell Street, East Hartford, 1893. This was one of four fire houses established that same year. A huge bell in the center of town would ring, alerting volunteers. The number of rings would indicate the location of the fire. East Hartford was previously serviced by the Hartford Fire Department until a water supply was piped in from Glastonbury.
COURTESY HISTORICAL SOCIETY OF EAST HARTFORD

ABOVE: Fifth Company, Hartford Police Department, Bushnell Park, Hartford, 1915. COURTESY PATTY D'AMOTO

RIGHT: Company E of the Connecticut State Guard assembled on the steps of the new East Hartford High School on Chapman Street. The State Guard provided security at home while the National Guard was serving in France. The company commander was Capt. Lewis B. Comstock. COURTESY HISTORICAL SOCIETY OF EAST HARTFORD

ABOVE: Members of the Connecticut State Guard, Hartford, 1919. First Lieutenant Mullens, Captain Cosgrove and Second Lieutenant Willis are identified. COURTESY CONNECTICUT STATE LIBRARY / #PICTURE GROUP 200, CONNECTICUT STATE GOVERNMENT, INSTITUTIONS AND PARKS, 1878-1973 GOVERNMENT BUILDINGS, STATE PARKS & OFFICIALS, BOX 1 OF 3

LEFT: A New Britain postman. COURTESY NEW BRITAIN INDUSTRIAL MUSEUM, DIV. OF NEW BRITAIN INSTITUTE

BELOW: Members of the Third Liberty Loan committee, New Britain, 1918. COURTESY NEW BRITAIN INDUSTRIAL MUSEUM, DIV. OF NEW BRITAIN INSTITUTE

ABOVE: A Hartford Fire Department firefighter and fire truck. COURTESY DONALD JACOBS

RIGHT: A postcard of a Hartford Police patrol wagon. COURTESY CONNECTICUT STATE LIBRARY / #PICTURE GROUP 800 POSTCARDS, CONNECTICUT HARTFORD-KILLINGWORTH BOX 6

OPPOSITE: Men on Quaker Hose Company No. 3 fire truck, West Hartford, 1921. COURTESY NOAH WEBSTER HOUSE AND WEST HARTFORD HISTORICAL SOCIETY

Governor Hiram Bingham III (seated, left) and Lieutenant Governor John H. Trumbull (seated, right) with the Governor's Foot Guards in the background, Hartford. 1925. Bingham was elected governor in November 1924. On December 16, 1924, Bingham was also elected as a Republican to serve in the United States Senate to fill a vacancy created by the death of Frank Bosworth Brandegee. Bingham defeated his opponent handily. Now both governor-elect and senator-elect, Bingham served as governor for one day, the shortest term of any Connecticut governor.

ABOVE: Connecticut State Firemen in front of the Comstock Building, Main Street, East Hartford, August 16, 1929. The firemen were in town for a convention.
COURTESY HISTORICAL SOCIETY OF EAST HARTFORD

LEFT: East Hartford Police Department on the steps of the High School on Chapman Street, 1928.
COURTESY RAYMOND LIBRARY COLLECTION

ABOVE: Captain Harry E. Generous of the 118th Observation Squadron Air Force, Brainard Field, Hartford, May 11, 1930. Captain Generous was a resident of East Hartford.
COURTESY HISTORICAL SOCIETY OF EAST HARTFORD

ABOVE RIGHT: Alfred W. Baldini, with meal in hand, in the first Civilian Conservation Corp Camp in Connecticut, Middlesex County, 1933. The CCC was part of the Public Works program started by President Franklin Roosevelt targeting families and veterans during the Great Depression.
COURTESY BALDINI FAMILY

RIGHT: The Windsor Fire Department Union Street firehouse, late 1930s. The firehouse was built in 1927.
COURTESY WINDSOR HISTORICAL SOCIETY, WINDSOR, CT / #2018.1.289

The Windsor Fire Company at the state's tercentenary celebration, fall of 1933. Edward Garvin is fourth from the left.

CHAPTER SEVEN

Community

Connecticut began and expanded as a parochial-minded place, with each community centered on its own Congregational church.

Immigration changed the state's religious, ethnic, and racial complexion, but home rule in 169 municipalities remained dominant and each new group of residents built lifelong bonds to towns, villages, neighborhoods, and parishes.

The English came to New Britain first, the Irish were next—followed by Germans, Swedes, Eastern Europeans, etc. The Polish were the last great wave of the nineteenth century, Puerto Ricans were the last wave of the twentieth.

Sacred Heart Church on Broad Street is in the heart of the city's Polish section. The church's website—www.sacredheartnb.org— lists statistics from the twentieth century's first decade to show how quickly the parish grew. In that time, priests conducted two marriages and five baptisms a week.

Polish-Americans changed the city with their language and culture and the addition of their energy to city businesses and public service.

Jewish immigrants changed Hartford and West Hartford. The first Jews, mostly from Germany, came to Hartford in the 1840s. Persecution in Russia prompted an influx of Eastern European Jews in the late nineteenth and early twentieth centuries.

Temple Beth Israel at 21 Charter Oak Avenue was the first building constructed in the state for use as a synagogue. George Keller, an Irish immigrant and Hartford's leading nineteenth-century architect, designed the building to resemble prominent Reform temples in Germany and New York City. The synagogue was dedicated in 1876 with a membership of 78.

In the 1930s, a few Jews began to leave Albany Avenue and other Hartford neighborhoods for nearby West Hartford, at the time a farming community, according to local historian Betty N. Hoffman. By the 1960s, many more Jews had pulled up stakes for the suburbs.

African Americans began coming to Hartford during the great migration out of the South in the early twentieth century. Many worked in the area's factories, and, like West Indians, they also labored in shade tobacco fields that were especially prevalent in Windsor. African Americans,

Jamaicans, and other immigrants from the Caribbean concentrated in Hartford's North End and the city's northern suburbs.

Italians settled in the city's South End, especially along Franklin Avenue. When the rush to the suburbs began in the 1950s and '60s, it was only natural for Italian-Americans to head for Wethersfield.

Through all the changes, the region's old Yankee families held onto their enclaves. Among the best known of the private clubs for the well-heeled and powerful was The Hartford Club on Prospect Street, founded in 1873.

Described in a *Courant* story as a "hideaway where men could discuss their business and political interests privately," the club's list of guests over the decades included Presidents Benjamin Harrison, William McKinley, and George H. W. Bush, along with Buffalo Bill and Walter Cronkite.

For many years an all-white, male bastion, the club admitted its first black member in 1971, and Hartford developer and business owner Richard Weaver-Bey became its first black president in 1999.

OPPOSITE: William Gillette in the attic room of his parent's home with two stationary engines he built as a child, Forest Street, Nook Farm, circa 1901. Gillette became famous for his portrayal of Sherlock Holmes on the stage and later built Seventh Sister, known as Gillette Castle now a state museum and park in Hadlyme, Connecticut. COURTESY HARRIET BEECHER STOWE CENTER

RIGHT: Painting of Noah Webster Jr. at age 75. Webster was an American founding father, lexicographer, textbook pioneer, English-language spelling reformer, political writer, editor, and prolific author. He was a strong supporter of the American Revolution and the ratification of the United States Constitution. Webster's name has become synonymous with "dictionary" in the United States. The modern Merriam-Webster dictionary is a direct descendant of Webster's original dictionary, *An American Dictionary of the English Language*, published in 1828. His *Grammatical Institute of the English Language* (aka The Blue Backed Speller), published in 1783, was a best-seller and taught millions of Americans how to be American. He has been called the "Father of American Scholarship and Education." COURTESY NOAH WEBSTER HOUSE AND WEST HARTFORD HISTORICAL SOCIETY

OPPOSITE: The Charter Oak with Honorable I. W. Stuart, Frederick Lawrence, and Nelson A. Moore, Hartford. COURTESY CONNECTICUT STATE LIBRARY / #PICTURE GROUP 400, HARTFORD COLLECTIONS, 1885-1936, BUILDING-DRUGSTORES, BOX 2 OF 5

RIGHT: Samuel Langhorne Clemens, circa 1883. Clemens, who was known by his pen name, Mark Twain, and his family lived in Hartford from 1871 to 1891. They lived in The Mark Twain House from 1874 to 1891.
COURTESY THE MARK TWAIN HOUSE & MUSEUM

ABOVE: Harriet Beecher Stowe seated at the front parlor desk of her Forest Street home, Nook Farm, August 18, 1886. Stowe was the internationally famous author of antislavery novel *Uncle Tom's Cabin*, published in 1852. She wrote 30 other novels and various articles on topics including antislavery and women's rights. Her home is a National Historic Landmark museum and program center open to the public. COURTESY HARRIET BEECHER STOWE CENTER

LEFT: Friends sit on steps of the Wells House, south of 38 Prospect Street, Nook Farm, circa 1885. Those pictured include the Clark, Perkins, Webb, Weld, and Riddle children. COURTESY HARRIET BEECHER STOWE CENTER

ABOVE: Installation of officers for the International Order of Odd Fellows (Swedish Chapter), Lodge No. 67, Hartford, April 18, 1893. Edward Setterberg is pictured middle row, second from right. COURTESY BARBARA BURNS TANGUAY

ABOVE RIGHT: Ruins of the Park Central Hotel after a boiler exploded, Hartford, February 1889. COURTESY CONNECTICUT STATE LIBRARY / #PICTURE GROUP 400, HARTFORD COLLECTIONS, 1885-1936, BUILDING-DRUGSTORES, BOX 2 OF 5

RIGHT: Mary Perkins, Mrs. Charles E. Perkins, and Lucy Perkins, 49 Woodland Street, Hartford, circa 1890. COURTESY HARRIET BEECHER STOWE CENTER

George Warner, friend Harriet W. Foote Taylor, wife Elisabeth Gillette Warner, and niece Margaret Warner Morley, in the Gillette House attic, Forest Street, Nook Farm, Winter 1893–94. COURTESY HARRIET BEECHER STOWE CENTER

ABOVE: Goodwin children in front of the family home, West Hartford. The family owned Goodwin Pottery. COURTESY NOAH WEBSTER HOUSE AND WEST HARTFORD HISTORICAL SOCIETY

ABOVE RIGHT: Family residence in Meadows floodplain, Darlin Street, East Hartford, April 9, 1901. Spring flooding of the Connecticut River was a nearly annual event prior to dike construction. COURTESY HISTORICAL SOCIETY OF EAST HARTFORD

RIGHT: Children gather at the Hayden Station Social Club, Windsor, 1894. Bessie Allen is the second girl from left in the second row. Owen W. Hayden is the small boy standing just behind her with dark bow tie. Alice Terry is the teacher on the far right of the back row. The club and former school was for activities including plays, parties, chapel, Sunday school, and library. COURTESY WINDSOR HISTORICAL SOCIETY, WINDSOR, CT / #1991.21.2.1

OPPOSITE: The laying of the cornerstone of Center Church House, 60 Gold Street, Hartford, 1909. The building was a memorial by the Cooley family to Charles Cooley, Hartford resident and Center Church member. COURTESY CENTER CHURCH, FIRST CHURCH OF CHRIST

Funeral procession of Governor George L. Lilley, Hartford, 1909. COURTESY CONNECTICUT STATE LIBRARY / #PICTURE GROUP 400 HARTFORD COLLECTION 1885-1936, PARADES & PROCESSIONS-RESIDENTS, BOX 4 OF 5

LEFT: The Ados Israel Choir, Hartford, circa 1914. Rabbi Issac Hurewitz was the first Orthodox rabbi in Hartford and the first spiritual leader of Ados Israel. Rabbi Hurewitz was the editor of the Yiddish publication the *Jewish Voice* and established many Jewish charitable and educational institutions. The choir was led by conductor Joseph Brown who also taught violin.
COURTESY JEWISH HISTORICAL SOCIETY OF GREATER HARTFORD

BELOW LEFT: Charles E. Perkins at his office, 14 State Street, Hartford, circa 1914. COURTESY HARRIET BEECHER STOWE CENTER

BELOW: Members of the Old Hartford Wheel Club gather together at the club's first reunion, Hartford, 1915.
COURTESY SUZANNE MILLER

ABOVE: Red Cross Parade, West Main and Cedar Streets, New Britain, May 18, 1918. COURTESY GLAESER FAMILY COLLECTION, NEW BRITAIN INDUSTRIAL MUSEUM, DIV. OF NEW BRITAIN INSTITUTE / #GLAESER FAMILY COLLECTION

LEFT: Sacred Heart School students in costume for the Red Cross Parade, New Britain, May 18, 1918. COURTESY NEW BRITAIN INDUSTRIAL MUSEUM, DIV. OF NEW BRITAIN INSTITUTE

OPPOSITE: Cornerstone laying ceremonies for the Morgan Memorial, part of The Wadsworth Atheneum, Hartford. The group included officials of the Morgan Memorial and state and city. COURTESY CONNECTICUT STATE LIBRARY / #PICTURE GROUP 400, BOX 2

ABOVE: Mary Monteith and George Keller, a famous Hartford architect noted for his Modern Gothic style, stand in front of Park Terrace, Hartford, 1920s. Keller designed the row houses in 1895 and made his home there. COURTESY HARRIET BEECHER STOWE CENTER

ABOVE RIGHT: Charles Brewer on the family farm on High Street, East Hartford, 1919. COURTESY AL BREWER FAMILY ARCHIVE

RIGHT: Tennis court in the garden behind the Perkins home, 38 Prospect Street, Nook Farm, Hartford. From left: Mabel Perkins, (Lucy) Weld, Henry and Edward Perkins. COURTESY HARRIET BEECHER STOWE CENTER

OPPOSITE: Boy Scout Troop 22 in front of St. Peters Church, Main Street, Hartford, circa 1927. Victor G. Muzzulin Jr. is pictured second row, fourth from right. COURTESY VICTOR MUZZULIN FAMILY

ABOVE: Katharine Seymour Day in her parlor, 73 Forest Street, Nook Farm, 1932. Day, a grandniece of Harriet Beecher Stowe, founded the Stowe Center in 1941 in order to preserve the home and her great aunt's legacy. She worked hard to promote civic improvements and historic preservation in Hartford, serving on the board of The Mark Twain House and Museum. COURTESY HARRIET BEECHER STOWE CENTER

RIGHT: Shoeshine boy Dominic LaMonica on Front Street, Hartford, circa 1932. COURTESY DONALD LAMONICA

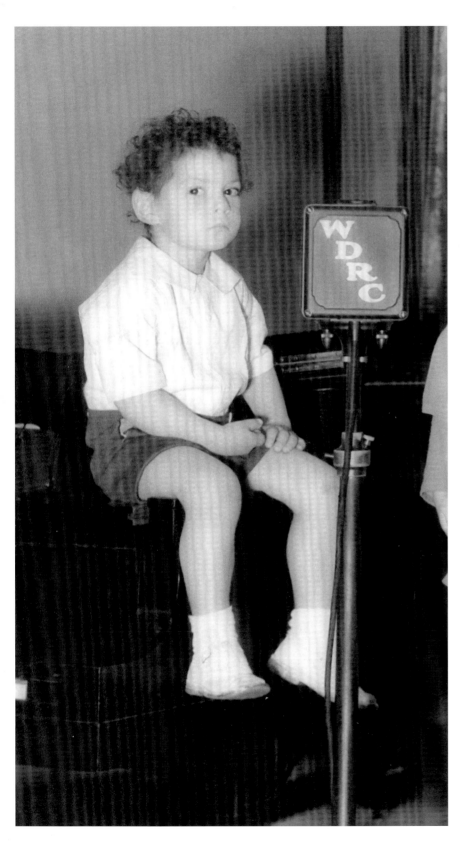

ABOVE: Mark Twain with family and friends outside his Hartford house, 1875. From left: Dr. A. Reeves Jackson, Susy Clemens, Samuel Clemens, Olivia Clemens, Mrs. Dr. A. Reeves Jackson. Dr. Jackson was the physician aboard the steamship *Quaker City*, which Mark Twain later traveled on when working as a journalist between June and November 1876.
COURTESY THE MARK TWAIN HOUSE & MUSEUM

FAR LEFT: Donald Cagenello sits in front of a WDRC radio microphone during the station's children's program, Hartford, 1933.
COURTESY DONALD CAGENELLO

LEFT: The Del Mastro family at Keney Park, Hartford, 1936. Esterina Del Mastro is pictured with her children (from left) Antonette, Patsy, Benny, and Maria.
COURTESY DEL MASTRO FAMILY

RIGHT: Jean Ramsdell with her bicycle, Windsor, 1937. COURTESY LEE ALLAN TRYON

FAR RIGHT: Alexander Duhansky and Vilma Hipsky on the day of their wedding engagement, Moose Meadow, Willington, 1936. COURTESY DIANA DUHANSKY MCVICKER

BELOW RIGHT: Family farm dogs take refuge from floodwaters on the roof of the Christensen family farmhouse, Meadow Road, Wilson area of Windsor, 1936. COURTESY CHRISTENSEN FAMILY

ABOVE: *Hartford Courant* sports editor Bill Lee, 1939. Lee replaced Bert Keane following Keane's death in 1939. COURTESY JEFF LEE

LEFT: The first Cathedral of Saint Joseph, Farmington Avenue, Hartford, 1937. The church was destroyed by fire in 1956. COURTESY ARCHDIOCESE OF HARTFORD / GEO. E. MEYERS

CHAPTER EIGHT

Recreation and Celebration

Connecticut people are justifiably proud of their University of Connecticut basketball champions.

But those are not the first teams in the state to amaze, and sad to say, disappoint.

Aetna fielded a women's basketball team that in 10 years, starting in 1924, racked up a UConn-like record of 111 wins and 22 losses.

The "Aetna Life Girls" played teams from Massachusetts to Illinois and Canada, as well as the best in Connecticut. At one point, the team had a 25-game winning streak. The Aetna women "consistently out-drew the leading men's teams of Central Connecticut," *The Courant* reported in a 1934 story.

The age of the players, family responsibilities, and a shortage of replacements contributed to the team's disbandment in 1934, former *Courant* sports editor Jeff Otterbein wrote in a "Moments in History" story on the newspaper's 250th anniversary in 2014.

The Hartford Dark Blues had a shorter history that will sound familiar to Hartford hockey fans. Formed in the 1870s, the Blues were a charter member of the National Association of Professional Base Ball Players, which eventually became the National League.

The team's field was on Wyllys Street on land owned by Elizabeth Colt near the Church of the Good Shepherd. The largest crowd in Dark Blues history, about 10,000, saw them go down to the Boston Red Stockings 10-5 on May 18, 1875.

In March 1877, seven weeks before the start of the second National League baseball season, team president Morgan Bulkeley, who also served as Hartford's mayor and state governor, announced the team was moving to Brooklyn. Hartford had been deemed unacceptable as a major league market.

"So there it was," *Courant* reporter Paul Doyle wrote in 2014, "120 years before Peter Karmanos uprooted the Whalers from Connecticut's capital city," Hartford's debut as a major league sports market was over after one season.

Here's justice, though: the Brooklyn Hartfords played only that season before folding.

Besides sports, turn-of-the century residents also turned to amusement parks modeled on the success of New York City's Coney Island. Luna Park in West Hartford, built on 12 acres where the Home Depot store on New Park Avenue now sits, opened in 1906 and featured a mile-long rollercoaster called the Scenic Railway.

"Also popular were a Ferris wheel, a merry-go-round, an 'Old Mill' tunnel of love, and a giant centrifuge called the 'circle swing' that twirled daredevils high above the ground," Trinity College Prof. Gene Leach wrote in a 2013 article for *Connecticut Explored* magazine (https://www.ctexplored.org/sample-article-the-scandalous-luna-park/).

The park, which sat next to a racetrack, closed in 1910 after only four years, in part, Leach wrote, because it was deemed "too risqué, too sporty" for prim Connecticut. West Hartford selectmen at one point objected to movie showings on Sundays.

"Young people, males in particular, loved Luna for its speed, sensualism, and exotic airs..." Leach wrote. "But park proprietors struggled to attract the middle class and the middle-aged."

OPPOSITE: A large contingent of draftees, headed by the Volunteer Band, leave for Camp Meade down Main Street, Hartford, June 24, 1918.
COURTESY CONNECTICUT STATE LIBRARY / #PICTURE GROUP 400 HARTFORD COLLECTION 1885-1936, PARADES & PROCESSIONS-RESIDENTS, BOX 4 OF 5

ABOVE: The Hartford Dark Blues baseball team of 1876. Front row: Dick Higham, Jack Burdock, Jack Remsen, Doug Allison. Second row: Tom Carey, Everrett Mills, Bob Ferguson, Bill Harbridge, Tommy York. Back row: Tommy Bond, Candy Cummings. The team played at the Hartford Ball Club Grounds and in 1876 they joined the National League as a charter member. The team's owner, Morgan G. Bulkeley, was also the first president of the National League. Managed by their third baseman, Bob Ferguson, the Dark Blues went on to finish third in 1876 with a record of 47–21.

OPPOSITE: Croquet game on the lawn of John and Isabella Beecher Hooker's Forest Street home, Nook Farm, circa 1870. From left: unidentified child with dog, John Hooker, Elisabeth G. Warner, Isabella Beecher Hooker, Charles Dudley Warner, Alice Hooker Day, Mary Hooker Burton.

Windsor Athletic Association team, 1895. COURTESY WINDSOR HISTORICAL SOCIETY, WINDSOR, CT / #2018.1.290

LEFT: Charles E. Perkins and Mary Russell Perkins with four unidentified friends picnic in the meadow behind 49 Woodland Street, Hartford, circa 1900. COURTESY HARRIET BEECHER STOWE CENTER

BELOW FAR LEFT: Putnam Phalanx headquarters (Armory), 265 Main Street, just south of Pearl Street, Hartford, circa 1879. Patriotic decorations indicate Battle Flag Day, September 17, 1879. COURTESY CONNECTICUT STATE LIBRARY / #PICTURE GROUP 400 HARTFORD COLLECTION 1885-1936, PARADES & PROCESSIONS-RESIDENTS, BOX 4 OF 5

BELOW LEFT: Parade festivities around the visit of President Benjamin Harrison, July 13, 1889. COURTESY CONNECTICUT STATE LIBRARY / #PICTURE GROUP 400 HARTFORD COLLECTION 1885-1936, PARADES & PROCESSIONS-RESIDENTS, BOX 4 OF 5

RIGHT: The Colt Fire Arms Band at Luna Park, West Hartford. COURTESY DONALD JACOBS

BELOW RIGHT: President Theodore Roosevelt visits Hartford, August 22, 1902. Roosevelt, the first president to ride in an automobile, is shown in a special electric automobile provided for the occasion. He is accompanied by Col. Jacob L. Green, president of the Connecticut Mutual Life Insurance Company. COURTESY CONNECTICUT STATE LIBRARY / #PICTURE GROUP 400 HARTFORD COLLECTION 1885-1936, PARADES & PROCESSIONS-RESIDENTS, BOX 4 OF 5

OPPOSITE: Poquonock baseball team, 1902. COURTESY WINDSOR HISTORICAL SOCIETY, WINDSOR, CT / #2010.39.66

ABOVE: John Grogan and Catherine (Dowd) Grogan's wedding day photo, Clinton Street, Hartford, July 1, 1907. Wedding party also included James Grogan, best man on left; Della Dowd, bridesmaid on right. John was a former captain of Company H, First Regiment, Connecticut National Guard and a veteran of the Spanish American war. He went on to serve as a member of the West Hartford Board of Fire Commissioners and West Hartford town council, was former chairman of the West Hartford police commission and at the time of his death at age 50 he was President of Hartford's Royal Typewriter's Foremen's Club. COURTESY JODI FYFE

LEFT: The midway at Luna Park, Hartford, circa 1908. The park offered a Ferris wheel, a miniature train ride, and numerous other attractions. COURTESY NOAH WEBSTER HOUSE AND WEST HARTFORD HISTORICAL SOCIETY

ABOVE: A postcard of Rockrimmon Lodge, Higganum. COURTESY CONNECTICUT STATE LIBRARY / #PG800 POSTCARDS, CONNECTICUT GREENWICH-HARTFORD BOX 4

ABOVE RIGHT: Colt's Patent Fire Arms Manufacturing Company float entry for the Bridge Dedication Parade, Hartford, October 7, 1908. COURTESY CONNECTICUT STATE LIBRARY / #PICTURE GROUP 460 COLT'S PATENT FIREARMS MANUFACTURING, BOX 4

RIGHT: Members of the West Hartford Glee Club, May 26, 1911. COURTESY NOAH WEBSTER HOUSE AND WEST HARTFORD HISTORICAL SOCIETY

A carnival in Avon, 1912. COURTESY DONALD JACOBS

ABOVE: C. J. Hill Co. employee outing, East Haddam, July 16, 1915. Frank Froebel is pictured in the front row, eighth person in from the right.
COURTESY EUGENE FROEBEL

RIGHT: The Ben Hurs champion basketball team, 1914–1915. Edward Louis Shieber Sr. is pictured in the third row, second from left.
COURTESY MARILYN (SHIEBER) SULLIVAN

ABOVE: Harness racing at the Berlin Fairgrounds, September 1917.
COURTESY GLAESER FAMILY COLLECTION,
NEW BRITAIN INDUSTRIAL MUSEUM,
DIV. OF NEW BRITAIN INSTITUTE /
#GLAESER FAMILY COLLECTION

LEFT: Soldiers marching in the Red Cross Parade, West Main Street, New Britain, May 18, 1918.
COURTESY GLAESER FAMILY COLLECTION,
NEW BRITAIN INDUSTRIAL MUSEUM,
DIV. OF NEW BRITAIN INSTITUTE /
#GLAESER FAMILY COLLECTION

Arthur Glaeser (third from left) and friends ski Shuttle Meadow golf course, January 20, 1918. COURTESY PAUL GLAESER COLLECTION / NEW BRITAIN INDUSTRIAL MUSEUM, DIV. OF NEW BRITAIN INSTITUTE / #PAUL GLAESER

LEFT: Postcard of Red Cross Parade, Main Street, Hartford, May 18, 1918. COURTESY DONALD JACOBS

BELOW: Members of the Hartford Wheel Club at the club's third reunion, Lake Compounce, Bristol, October 7, 1918. COURTESY SUZANNE MILLER

RIGHT: Ellen Stone Elmer stands on the running board of a patriotically decorated truck parked in front of the Elmer Ford Agency, Trumbull Street, Hartford, circa 1919. The Ford dealership was owned by Ellen's parents, Lucius Harmon Elmer and Ada Kalish Elmer. COURTESY SUZANNE MILLER

BELOW RIGHT: Postcard of the Governor's Foot Guard and a contingent of Hartford policemen on parade, Hartford. COURTESY DONALD JACOBS

OPPOSITE: A crowd of 4,000 people listen to the returns from the Jack Dempsey-Georges Carpentier fight outside the *Courant* newspaper office, July 2, 1921. The fight was billed as "The Fight of the Century." COURTESY CONNECTICUT STATE LIBRARY / #PICTURE GROUP 400 HARTFORD COLLECTION 1885-1936, RESTAURANTS-TROLLEYS, BOX 5 OF 5

RIGHT: A. C. Petersen Farms Dairy employees line up with parade entries for the original "Park Road Parade," 240 Park Road, West Hartford, circa 1923. Andrew C. Petersen can be seen left of center, holding the reins of one of the horses.
COURTESY THE PETERSEN FAMILY

BELOW: School children represent the state's various counties parade at the State Fair grounds, West Hartford, circa 1925.
COURTESY NOAH WEBSTER HOUSE AND WEST HARTFORD HISTORICAL SOCIETY

OPPOSITE TOP LEFT: Auto racing action, State Fair, West Hartford, 1926. The car behind the car in front crashed into the grandstands. COURTESY NOAH WEBSTER HOUSE AND WEST HARTFORD HISTORICAL SOCIETY

OPPOSITE TOP RIGHT: Connecticut State Fair parade, Main Street by the old State House, Hartford, 1926.
COURTESY NOAH WEBSTER HOUSE AND WEST HARTFORD HISTORICAL SOCIETY

OPPOSITE BOTTOM RIGHT: A harness race at the State Fair, West Hartford, circa 1925. COURTESY NOAH WEBSTER HOUSE AND WEST HARTFORD HISTORICAL SOCIETY

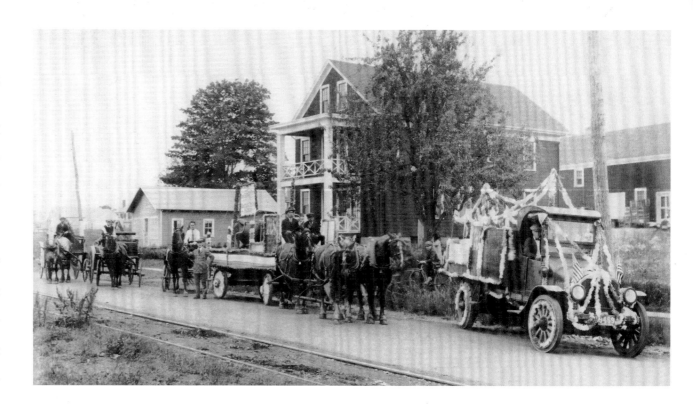

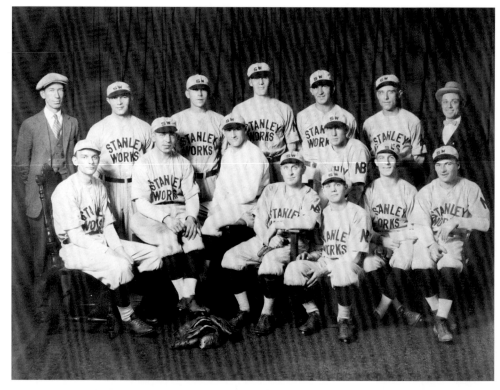

ABOVE: The Young Women's Hebrew Association basketball team, Hartford, 1931. The team competed in the Hartford County Women's League, which included the YWCA, Aetna Life, and teams from Simsbury. Dr. Morris Cohen was the manager.
COURTESY JEWISH HISTORICAL SOCIETY OF GREATER HARTFORD

ABOVE RIGHT: The Stanley Works baseball team, New Britain, 1926.
COURTESY NEW BRITAIN INDUSTRIAL MUSEUM, DIV. OF NEW BRITAIN INSTITUTE

RIGHT: P. F. Corbin Company women's basketball team, New Britain, 1928. COURTESY NEW BRITAIN INDUSTRIAL MUSEUM, DIV. OF NEW BRITAIN INSTITUTE

The Eddie Allen Dance Orchestra, Old Town Hall Inn and Diner, East Hartford, late 1930s. The band included: Seymour Rosenberg, Evie (Everett) Vale, Eddie Allen Handleman, Sy Quinto. Eddie was the leader and trumpet player. COURTESY JOSEPH A. HANDLEMAN

Ahern Funeral Homes

Our History

The Ahern Funeral Home, Inc. was founded in 1886 by J.J. Ahern and Francis Ahern in the city of Hartford, on the corner of Main and Pearl. Later, the funeral home was moved to 100 Pearl Street, where the business was conducted until 1906, when they built the first building used specifically for funeral services in the city of Hartford at 101 Chapel Street.

In 1934, The Ahern Funeral Home moved to its current location at 180 Farmington Avenue, where the business was operated by the nephews of the two founders, brothers Francis R.Ahern and Albert T.Ahern.

Ahern Funeral Home remains today in the same location, under the supervision of Francis R. Ahern's children, Francis R. Ahern and Sarah Ahern-Jordan.

In 1974, the Ahern family expanded their operation with the purchase of an additional funeral home in Unionville, Connecticut. The Unionville location services the Farmington Valley.

The Ahern Funeral Home has been family-owned and operated and has served the greater Hartford area for three generations.

Ahern Funeral Home is a family owned and operated business located in the greater Hartford area for more than 125 years. Established in 1886, we have two locations — Hartford and Unionville, Connecticut. We are committed to offering the best funeral services to families in our community.

The Bushnell Center
for the Performing Arts

The history of The Bushnell is a story of love between a father and
a daughter...and their mutual love of their hometown of Hartford.
Both Horace Bushnell and his daughter, Dotha Bushnell Hillyer, who
conceived and built The Bushnell as a permanent tribute to her father,
left indelible imprints on the Capitol City. Their individual visions and
collective contributions have benefited and changed the lives of multiple
generations of Connecticut citizens.

Inspired by a 1912 visit to Springfield's new municipal auditorium,
Dotha developed her own dream for Hartford. She envisioned a world-class
performing arts center downtown, which would both serve as a memorial
to her beloved father and as "a gift to the people of Connecticut....
a center for the benefit of arts, science and community activities."

With uncanny savvy, she hired Corbett, Harrison and MacMurray, two
years before these innovative architects designed Radio City Music Hall,
and sold her stock in December of 1928 – a brilliant stroke of market
timing – to begin construction in 1929. In 1930, The Bushnell opened,
being heralded as a "beacon of hope," in the midst of the Depression –
such it has remained for nearly 90 years.

And, now, we continue to be a community gathering space, bringing
Connecticut audiences face-to-face with the world's finest musicians,
authors, orchestras, dance companies, theater and many other
special presentations.

Dotha Bushnell Hillyer

Horace Bushnell

Mortensen Hall

THE
BUSHNELL

Charter Oak
CULTURAL CENTER
art that moves the world

Charter Oak Cultural Center

A Master Plan is in place to restore, expand and improve the Center's spaces, inside and out, for the benefit of local and regional visitors

A Fight for Religious Liberty

Hartford's early Jewish residents poured their heart and soul into constructing a building that would stand as a vivid testament to their faith and their community.

Their struggle is also the story of America's struggle to expand civil rights and religious freedom. When it opened its doors in 1876, Temple Beth Israel on Charter Oak Avenue became the first building in Connecticut's history to be constructed specifically as a synagogue. They also built an architectural masterpiece, a timeless symbol of Victorian-Moorish style and grandeur, created by famed Hartford architect George Keller.

To create this unique house of worship, Hartford's early Jewish immigrants waged a decades-long battle to overcome state laws prohibiting formal Jewish religious assembly. In many ways, the building itself is a testament to one of New England's earliest civil rights battles – the right to worship freely.

A Time of Transition and Renewal

Fast forward more than 100 years to the late 1970s. Hartford has undergone enormous change. Long-abandoned as a synagogue, this once proud building faced demolition when a group of pioneering Jewish leaders successfully fought to save it. After a partial restoration was completed, these leaders believed that if the building and its legacy were going to survive, they needed to imbue it with new purpose. Just as Temple Beth Israel strengthened, inspired, and united the early Jewish community in Hartford a century ago, these advocates and organizers believed that a new multi-cultural arts center would help to strengthen, inspire, and unite the diverse communities that now call Hartford home. Charter Oak Cultural Center was born.

A New Kind of Community Arts Organization

Founded in 1979 to breathe new life into the abandoned Temple Beth Israel building, Charter Oak Cultural Center is now the leading presenter of multi-cultural visual and performing arts and the main provider of free arts education to underserved youth in the Hartford region. As part of its mission to do the work of social justice through the arts, Charter Oak also offers ground-breaking programs designed to meet critical community needs.

Curating and Presenting Visual and Performing Arts

Located on the upper level, Charter Oak's Sanctuary is a 180-seat performing arts center which showcases a wide range of multi-cultural performances and events. On the ground level, the Gallery hosts provocative visual art exhibits. To ensure art is truly accessible to all, no person is turned away who cannot afford a ticket.

Providing Arts Education to Hartford's Children

Charter Oak's Youth Arts Institute provides free, high quality arts education for over 1,000 underserved Hartford children. In 2013, the Youth Arts Institute was recognized by the White House for excellence in youth programming.

Incubating Innovative Social Programming

Whether it is chronic homelessness or strained relationship with the police, Charter Oak responds to community needs by incubating innovative programs that become national models. In these ways, this special place continues to serve as a guiding light for improving the lives of the overlooked and underserved.

Congregation Beth Israel, now Charter Oak Cultural Center, as it appeared just after opening in 1876.

21 Charter Oak Avenue
Hartford, CT 06061
www.charteroakcenter.org
(860) 249-1207

Index